MW00843621

BEST JUNIOR HANDLER!

A guide to showing successfully in Junior Showmanship

by **Anne Olejniczak & Denise Olejniczak**

Doral Publishing, Inc.
1997

Published by Doral Publishing, Inc.
Printed in the United States of America.

Edited by Luana Luther.
Cover by Color Tech and Graphica Pacific Design

Library of Congress Number: 95-71341
ISBN: 0-944875-45-9

Olejniczak, Anne.
      Best junior handler! : a guide to showing successfully in junior showmanship / by Anne Olejniczak & Denise Olejniczak. --
      Wilsonville, OR : Doral Pub., 1997.

      p. : ill. ; cm.

      Includes bibliographical references and
index.
        ISBN: 0-944875-45-9

       1. Dog shows--Junior showmanship classes--
Best junior handler.   I. Olejniczak,
Denise. II. Title.

SF425.13.0   636.7'08'88 dc20
                95-71341

To Muff, the one who started it all.
To Cricket, who made me a better handler.
To my Dad, who put up with a lot!

Acknowledgments

Sally Ann Helf and Jenny Drastura for their editing expertise and advice.

Ruth Dehmel for the artwork and photography.

Nancy Plunkett for the anatomy drawing.

John Cox for his research into the AKC Show Awards to update the Westminster winners.

Stephanie Lehman and her mom for the information on Crufts.

Tracie Laliberte for the photo and information on Crufts.

Ted Fahlgren for recruiting additional Canadian Kennel Club information and photos.

Gale Grey, Gene Grey and James Norris for their information on the German Shepherd.

Jerry Bently at Pedigree for the National Junior Showmanship Invitational Information.

Newport Dog Shows for the World Series Information.

Amy Andrews for filling in the gaps and her support.

Dr. Alvin Grossman and Doral Publishing for making this book possible.

To all the juniors and handlers who responded to our requests for photographs.

Special thanks to all the instructors and mentors who molded me into the handler that I am: Bill Pearce, Dick McKinney, Jim Maloney, Fred Dieball, Bob McRae, Jolene Cazzola, and Pat Martello.

Most of all thanks to all my Junior's dogs: Fluff, Toby, Chad, Classy, Buck, Boots, Willie, Heather, Michael and Cricket.

About the Authors

Anne Olejniczak competed for eight years in Junior Showmanship. During her career, she was a seven-time Westminster qualifier and competed three times. Anne was the only junior handler to qualify and compete with a Lhasa Apso at the World Series of Junior Showmanship. She was top Lhasa junior handler for seven consecutive years. In her last year of Junior Showmanship, Anne competed until she aged out in August of 1992 with a total of 15 Best Junior Handler wins and 17 first place wins. At the end of that year, she was still ranked number 12 junior handler—all breeds—in the United States, top Lhasa junior handler and runner-up junior handler in English Springer Spaniels even though she had competed for only 7 1/2 months.

In addition to competing in Junior Showmanship in 1992, Anne also finished three Lhasa Apsos, all three were completely breeder/owner/handled by her and finished with three majors, two of which with 5 point Specialty wins. She was awarded her first Group I that year with her English Springer Spaniel, the very first time they took Best of Breed.

Anne is now breeder/owner/handler for her Lhasas on a limited basis while attending college and pursuing a career in writing. She has written a regular column in the *The Lhasa Apso Reporter* on handling for the past five years. In 1993, she was presented the Junior Writers Award by the Dog Writer's Association of America.

Denise Olejniczak has been exhibiting and breeding Lhasa Apsos for more than 12 years. She is the editor and publisher of *The Lhasa Apso Reporter*, an international breed magazine and has written articles that have been published in *Dog World Magazine* and *The American Kennel Gazette*. In addition, Mrs. Olejniczak was licensed by the American Kennel Club to judge Junior Showmanship in 1993.

Foreword

When Anne and Denise Olejniczak asked me to write an introduction to *Best Junior Handler*, I accepted with mixed feelings: Mainly because I have never judged Junior Handling but have watched it being judged in many countries in the world. I accepted in spite of not having judged because maybe I had seen enough outside-looking-in to make me applaud it or not.

Junior Handling is important for many reasons. One of them is not just winning or losing, but learning how to play the game correctly and fairly. Learning and becoming familiar with winning and losing at an early age is very important. For a junior wishing to succeed, it should be easy—by studying the expression of the dogs whether they win or lose and shake their tails with the great pleasure of having pleased their handler.

To be able to handle a dog to advantage such as correct grooming, a comfortable and advantageous pace of movement and to stand for inpsection is quite an achievement. There are right and wrong ways of doing this and vary from breed to breed.

Experience is truly the best method providing you are aware of all the pitfalls. *Best Junior Handler* makes you aware of the pitfalls and tells you how to overcome them. This book can be of great help to any young person providing they always keep in mind that in their dog's eyes they are all the best.

Good luck and good reading.

—Nigel Aubrey-Jones

Preface

From the time I was a child, books have always played an important part in my life. As I grew older, my reading material was always extensive on whatever subject happened to fascinate me at the time. So naturally, when I began showing dogs in Junior Showmanship, I read what I could on what proved to be a very limited subject. As time passed and the rules for Junior Showmanship changed, the few good sources of information soon became outdated.

During my career as a junior handler, I was asked by several handlers to work for them. I always turned them down because I had my own breeder-owner handled Lhasas to show, and I did not want to give that up to pursue a handling career. Therefore, I was forced to learn many of the finer points of handling successfully in Junior Showmanship on my own. I also found that no amount of instruction from any one individual can replace the most important ingredient necessary for winning consistently in Junior Showmanship— teamwork. And, becoming a team with your dog can only be accomplished by regular practice sessions and personal interaction with your dog.

Anne at age two with Lassie, her first dog.

Now that I am retired from Junior Showmanship and attending college to become a writer, I have decided to utilize my skills and share my experiences with other junior handlers. My goal was to write a text book on Junior Showmanship that contained the basics for getting started in juniors, plus enough advanced work so that any junior, regardless of his level of experience, could learn to show more effectively. The result is this book, *Best Junior Handler!* This book differs from many of the others on junior showmanship in that has been solely devoted to the subject— junior showmanship. I did not include chapters on kennel management, health care (other than what would be routinely needed at shows) nor careers in dogs. I chose to devote every page of this book to some valuable aspect of junior showmanship. I hope you enjoy it and have as much fun in junior showmanship as I did!

—Anne Olejniczak

Anne Olejniczak and Ch. Cricket's Chirp shown winning their first Group One. Not only did Anne win the Group that day, but she was awarded Winners Bitch and Best of Breed in Lhasa Apsos and Best Junior Handler, which demonstrates the heights to which a junior can aspire. (Bill Meyer Photo)

Table of Contents

Chapter 1
What is Junior Showmanship?

Junior Showmanship is a preteen and teenage version of showing dogs in conformation events sponsored by national kennel clubs: the American Kennel Club (AKC), the Canadian Kennel Club (CKC), the Kennel Club of England and FCI clubs. It is a growing event

Kellie Herbel, pictured at age 9, winning Best of Winners with her Lhasa Apso.(Shirley Daigle Photo)

worldwide. In Junior Showmanship, the young exhibitor is given the opportunity to compete with individuals in his own age group in an organized manner at a dog show. This form of competition allows the junior handler to test and refine his handling skills and learn to build a strong working relationship with his dog. In addition, the young handler will learn to win and lose with dignity and grace. Many junior handlers graduate to the level of successful owner-handling and professional-handling careers and develop the handling techniques necessary to excel in Breed, Group and Best in Show competition.

In AKC-sanctioned shows, the Junior Showmanship classes are divided into four groups. The Novice classes are for those junior handlers who have not won three first place wins (with competition present). The Open classes are for those junior handlers who have won three first place wins in the Novice class. Novice and Open are divided into two age groups. The Junior division is for handlers who are at least 10 years old and under 14 years of age on the day of the show. The Senior division is for handlers who are at least 14 years old and under 18 years of age on the day of the show.

The divisions of Junior Showmanship classes are similar in other countries.

Chapter 2
Beginnings

The Dog

A dog shown in Junior Showmanship faces stress both physically and mentally. In many ways the Junior Showmanship dog leads the same life as the heavily campaigned specials dog. The vigorous schedule of show weekend after show weekend can break some dogs while others excel. The perfect Junior Showmanship dog is nonexistent. Each dog has his own quirks, but learning to deal with these quirks on a day-to-day basis is what makes successful junior handlers.

The best Junior Showmanship dog should meet three requirements. First, the dog must possess a stable personality. Stable is defined as not easily spooked or freaked by unexpected noises and activity. This does not mean that he must stand still like a little soldier the entire time he is

Training a dog for junior showmanship can begin in puppyhood.

being shown or that he performs all of his tasks perfectly. This paragon of perfection is difficult to find and showing a dog of this type does not necessarily demonstrate the junior handler's abilities. However, the dog must be able to be controlled by the junior handler.

Second, the dog must have stamina. Stamina, according to the *New Webster's Dictionary*, means a capacity for resisting fatigue. In other words, the dog does not get tired easily. A dog without stamina will not survive in Junior Showmanship. The dog will shut down and not want to show more often and could pose a problem for the junior handler if he does not own a backup dog.

The last quality necessary for a Junior Showmanship dog is reliability. A good Junior Showmanship dog should be reliable 75 to 80 percent of the time. You will not want to go into the ring with a dog you are not comfortable with because you don't know what he is going to do. This uncertainty will affect your confidence as well as your performance.

Attend Fun Matches and Dog Shows to Observe Junior Showmanship

To find out if Junior Showmanship is for you, observe an exhibition at a fun match or dog show. There are many ways to find local dog

Fun matches can be great practice.

shows. The breeder of your dog will be able to give you information. Some newspapers in larger metropolitan areas will list local dog shows, times, and locations in the entertainment sections. Magazines, such as *Dog World* and *Dog Fancy* (see Appendix) can be found in local book stores or are available by subscription. These magazines have listings in each issue for at least a month's schedule of shows with dates and who to contact for information.

The American Kennel Gazette (see Appendix for address), published by the AKC, is available at dog shows by subscription and in bookstores. This magazine has three sections: The *Gazette* with articles and AKC information is mailed with the Show Calendar and can be subscribed for separately or with the Show Awards which is mailed under separate cover. The Show Calendar has listings of all the dog shows for several months in advance with all the information needed to enter including blank entry forms.

Choosing the Breed

Choosing a breed of dog for Junior Showmanship can be a difficult decision. Not only do you have to find a breed that suits your personality, but also your living space. A sporting breed might be inappropriate if you live in a small apartment. A terrier might not be the best if a high energy level grates on your nerves.

The best way to find a dog is by picking out a few breeds you like. Then, learn about the breed, watch them at shows, and meet with the breeders to see what the dogs are like in their own environment. This careful assessment will give you a good idea of what will fit your needs and your lifestyle.

Purchasing a dog is an important decision that will affect your life as well as the dog's. Never make an emotional choice or a quick decision because of pressure. Take your time and choose wisely.

Once you have chosen a breed, establish yourself with a breeder who can teach you the grooming and handling techniques necessary for the breed. Most breeders will be happy to help you learn and excel in your new-found breed.

Training Classes

Now that you have the dog and the information on shows, your next step will be to learn how to show your dog. Training classes are available through many local kennel clubs or organizations. You might have to do a little investigation to find out what is available in your area if you do not have friends with show dogs who can direct you. Start by calling the local veterinarian, checking the yellow pages or the dog section of classified ads in your local newspaper. If you still are unable to find any training classes, contact AKC for the address of a list of local kennel clubs in your area. If you subscribe to *The American Kennel Gazette*, the addresses are listed at least once a year.

The cost of training classes will vary from three or four dollars for one class to 25 dollars or more for an eight-week session. Some kennel clubs offer them free of charge. As a beginner, you should try to attend class on a weekly basis. There is so much to learn, and you can never have too much practice time. Some training centers offer special classes for junior handlers. These classes are very nice to have, but I feel you will learn more by practicing with the adults.

The equipment you will need for training class should be what you will be using in the ring at the dog show. If you have a coated breed, you might want to take a brush or comb with you. Bring a variety of show leads to get a feel for what is right for you and the dog. These items can be picked up at shows, pet supply stores, wholesale outlets or through catalogs specializing in dogs.

Bait is also a must unless you have a dog that does not care for it. Cooked liver seasoned with garlic salt is the favored delicacy of many show dogs. Chicken, kidneys, beef or cheese can also be used according to your dog's preference. Many exhibitors use processed hot dogs made by Gerber® for babies or Vienna® Sausages or Hormel® Cocktail Weiners. Cat treats, such as Pounce® and Bonkers®, appeal to many dogs. Try out the different types of bait available on your dog at home and see what holds his attention the longest. Then take plenty with you to class.

Dressing for class is simple. Wear comfortable clothes, like slacks and T-shirts or sweatshirts. Your dog should be neat and clean, free of parasites and up to date on all his shots. If the weather is warm, bring something to drink, for yourself as well as for your dog, and a small hand towel. After all, you won't be the only one working hard!

Chapter 3
Beginning Your Junior Showmanship Career

Junior Showmanship Identification Number

As you approach the time to enter your first competition, you will need to apply to the American Kennel Club (see Appendix) for your Junior Showmanship Identification Number. This number will be used on all entry forms for the shows you enter. To receive your number, write to the AKC giving your name, address and birth date. Enclose a self-addressed stamped envelope for a speedier reply.

Eligibility of the Dog

To be eligible for Junior Showmanship, the dog must be owned or co-owned by the junior handler or a member of his immediate family (father, mother, brother, sister, uncle, aunt, grandfather, grandmother, including the corresponding step and half relations) or by a member of the junior handler's household.

The dog must be eligible to compete in Obedience or Conformation; however, *bitches in season may not be shown*. With the new rule changes in 1989, a junior handler may substitute another dog for the one entered (as long as he meets the ownership requirements) after entries close if there is a good and valid reason, such as a bitch entry coming in season. A veterinarian's excuse must be provided by the owner explaining the withdrawal of the original dog (i.e., illness or a bitch in season) as well as an entry form. All requests must be made one-half hour prior to judging of any regular classes at the show.

Heather Grodi show winning Best Junior Handler at the Puget Sound English Springer Spaniel Association Specialty. Specialty shows allow juniors to compete with others in the same breed.(Callea Photo)

Type of Shows

There are three types of AKC-approved shows. The All-Breed show is the most common event and provides judging for all breeds of dogs. At the All-Breed Show, dogs are only required to be there at the time of judging and may be taken home as soon as judging is over.

The Benched show is an all-day event. Entered dogs must remain at the show site on the benches provided by the superintendent during the regular show hours. The only exception is when the dog is being groomed or shown. At the Benched show, dogs may not leave the show site until they are formally excused by the superintendent.

A Specialty show provides judging for one breed or a group of breeds (i.e., Toy Group, Rare Breeds), and only dogs of that specific breed or breeds can be entered. There are no other special requirements for eligibility and the dogs may be brought in and out of the show site at any time.

The Premium List

Now that you have applied for an Identification Number, the next step is to contact the show superintendents and request to be put on their mailing lists. The show superintendents' addresses are listed in the *Gazette Show Calendar*, as well as in the Show Directory of *Dog World* and *Dog Fancy* magazines. You will then begin to receive the premium lists for shows in your vicinity.

A premium list provides all the necessary information about a show including the closing date, entry fee, location, hotels that will take dogs, prizes and entry forms. To enter the show, fill out the entry form on both sides as shown in Example A. When making out the entry form, it is advisable to have the dog's AKC Registration Papers handy or make a special record of the information if those papers are stored in a safe place. Once the form is complete, mail it to the superintendent with the appropriate fees at least a week before the listed closing date on the premium list.

Judging Program

About a week before the date of the show you have entered, you will receive a judging program and entry ticket. The entry ticket merely confirms your entry and provides you with your armband number. It will also serve as an admission ticket for you on the day of the show. If you have entered a benched show, you will be asked to show the ticket when bringing the dog in and out of the show site. This precaution is

Form A.

OFFICIAL AMERICAN KENNEL CLUB ENTRY FORM

SAMPLE FORM

Name of Show
Date of Show

I ENCLOSE $ __10__ for my entry fees.
IMPORTANT—Read Carefully Instructions on Reverse Side Before Filling Out. Numbers in the boxes indicate sections of the instructions relevant to the information needed in that box. (PLEASE PRINT)

BREED	VARIETY (1)	SEX
Scottish Deerhound		Male

DOG (2) (3) SHOW CLASS	CLASS (3) DIVISION Weight, Color, etc.	
ADDITIONAL CLASSES		
OBEDIENCE TRIAL CLASS	JR. SHOWMANSHIP CLASS	Open Senior

NAME OF (See Back)
JUNIOR HANDLER (if any)   Stephen Wallace

FULL NAME OF DOG   CH Stephen's Almighty

☒ AKC. REG. NO.	Enter number here	DATE OF BIRTH	5-22-93
☐ AKC. LITTER NO.	ZZ 500325/01		
☐ ILP NO.		PLACE OF BIRTH	☒ USA ☐ Canada ☐ Foreign
☐ FOREIGN REG NO. & COUNTRY			☐ Do not print the above in catalog

BREEDER   Owners

SIRE   CH MacAndrew's Bannockburn

DAM   CH Stephen's Crazy Maizy

| ACTUAL OWNER(S) | (Please Print) | ☐ OWNERSHIP CHANGE |
| (4) R. MacAndrew & S. Wallace | | |

| OWNER'S ADDRESS | Box 50 Route 1 | ☐ OWNERSHIP CHANGE or ☐ ADDRESS CHANGE |
| CITY Falkirk | STATE MN ZIP 23456 | ID# |

NAME OF OWNER'S AGENT
(IF ANY) AT THE SHOW

I CERTIFY that I am the actual owner of the dog, or that I am the duly authorized agent of the actual owner whose name I have entered above. In consideration of the acceptance of this entry, I (we) agree to abide by the rules and regulations of The American Kennel Club in effect at the time of this show or obedience trial or both, and by any additional rules and regulations appearing in the premium list for this show or obedience trial or both, and further agree to be bound by the Agreement printed on the reverse side of this entry form. I (we) certify and represent that the dog entered is not a hazard to persons or other dogs. This entry is submitted for acceptance on the foregoing representation and agreement.

SIGNATURE of owner or his agent
duly authorized to make this entry.

Telephone __505-555-2121__   Pers. ID Code # _____

AGREEMENT

I (we) acknowledge that the "Rules Applying to Registration and Dog Shows" and, if this entry is for an obedience trial, the "Obedience Regulations," have been made available to me (us), and that I am (we are) familiar with their contents. I (we) agree that the club holding this show or obedience trial has the right to refuse this entry for cause which the club shall deem to be sufficient. In consideration of the acceptance of this entry and of the holding of the show or obedience trial and of the opportunity to have the dog judged and to win prize money, ribbons, or trophies, I (we) agree to hold this club, its members, directors, governors, officers, agents, superintendents or show secretary and the owner or lessor of the premises and any employees of the aforementioned parties, harmless from any claim for loss or injury which may be alleged to have been caused directly or indirectly to any person or thing by the act of this dog while in or upon the show or obedience trial premises or grounds or near any entrance thereto, and I (we) personally assume all responsibility and liability for any such claim; and I (we) further agree to hold the aforementioned parties harmless from any claim for loss of this dog by disappearance, theft, death or otherwise, and from any claim for damage or injury to the dog, whether such loss, disappearance, theft, damage, or injury be caused or alleged to be caused by the negligence of the club or any of the parties aforementioned, or by the negligence of any other person, or any other cause or causes. I (we) hereby assume the sole responsibility for and agree to indemnify and save the aforementioned parties harmless from any and all loss and expense (including legal fees) by reason of the liability imposed by law upon any of the aforementioned parties for damage because of bodily injuries, including death at any time resulting therefrom, sustained by any person or persons, including myself (ourselves) or on account of damage to property, arising out of or in consequence of my (our) participation in this show or obedience trial, however such injury, death or damage to property may be caused, and whether or not the same may have been caused or may be alleged to have been caused by the negligence of the aforementioned parties or any of their employees or agents, or any other persons.

Single copies of the latest editions of the "Rules Applying to Registration and Dog Shows" and "Obedience Regulations" may be obtained WITHOUT CHARGE from any Superintendent at above where they are superintending or from THE AMERICAN KENNEL CLUB, 51 MADISON AVENUE, NEW YORK, NY 10015.

INSTRUCTIONS

1. (Variety) If you are entering a dog of a breed in which there are varieties for show purposes, please designate the particular variety you are entering i.e., Cocker Spaniel (solid color black, ASCOB, part-color), Beagles (not exceeding 13 in. over 13 in. but not exceeding 15 in.), Dachshunds (longhaired, smooth, wirehaired), Collies (rough, smooth), Bull Terriers (colored, white), Manchester Terriers (standard, toy), Chihuahuas (smooth coat, long coat), English Toy Spaniels (King Charles and Ruby, Blenheim and Prince Charles), Poodles (toy, miniature, standard)

2. The following categories of dogs may be entered and shown in Best of Breed competition: Dogs that are Champions of Record and dogs which according to their owners' records, have completed the requirements for a championship, but whose championships are unconfirmed. The showing of unconfirmed Champions, in Best of Breed competition is limited to a period of 90 days from the date of the show where this dog completed the requirements for a championship.

3. (Dog Show Class) Consult the classification in this premium list. If the dog show class in which you are entering your dog is divided, then, in addition to designating the class, specify the particular division of the class in which you are entering your dog, i.e., age, color, weight division.

4. A dog must be entered in the name of the person who actually owned it at the time entries for a show closed. If a registered dog has been acquired by a new owner, it must be entered in the name of its new owner in any show for which entries closed after the date of acquirement, regardless of whether the new owner has received the registration certificate indicating that the dog is recorded in his name. State on entry form whether transfer application has been mailed to A.K.C. (For complete rule refer to Chapter 14, Section 3.)

JUNIOR SHOWMANSHIP

If this entry is for a Jr. Showmanship, please give the following information:

AKC JUNIOR HANDLER NUMBER [0] [8] [0] [3] [4] [0] [0] [9]

JR.'S DATE OF BIRTH 8-3-84

The above number MUST be included. Should you not have your Junior Handler number, this may be obtained from the American Kennel Club. (Phone) 212-696-8345, 212-696-8240 or 212-696-8281.

ADDRESS __Same as on the front.__

CITY _____ STATE _____ ZIP _____

If Jr. Handler is not the owner of the dog identified on the face of this form, what is the relationship of the Jr. Handler to the owner? _____

taken to make sure you are not trying to steal the dog or bring in unentered dogs. **So don't throw it away**!

The judging program includes directions to the show site, judging times, the ring number you will be showing in, and the number of juniors entered. The easiest way to find Junior Showmanship information is to open the program to the index that is usually located on the inside cover. There you will find a listing of breeds in alphabetical order. Look under "J" and you will find Junior Showmanship. In front of the words Junior Showmanship, you will find a number. This is the total entry for juniors. You will find a ring number and time behind the words Junior Showmanship. Look for the ring number in the interior of the program and you will see the judge's name and his schedule. You will then find the break down of each Junior Showmanship class listed by the appropriate time. This schedule will make planning your day much easier and less hectic.

Equipment

The equipment needed for the show consists of the basics: grooming table, grooming arm (optional), tack box, your clothes, bait and weather gear. Your tack box should be filled with your grooming supplies, a spray bottle with fresh water (for your dog to drink in warm weather), hand towel and show leads. Your weather gear requirements are seasonal. When weather is wet from snow or rain, you may need extra towels for drying a wet dog. Regardless of the season, never leave without adequate rain gear for yourself (and possibly your dog) for outdoor shows.

Show Preparation

Your dog should be fully groomed and bathed before going to the show. Only quick show grooms and touch-ups should be done at the show site. This is less stressful and time consuming for both the dog and the handler.

A typical show groom consists of a quick once-over for short-coated breeds and a wet down and blow dry for longer-coated breeds. Some dogs require chalking and this should be done as needed. The finished picture should be neat and orderly. (A small note to those who must use chalk: Make sure you let your dog shake a few times or pat out the excess before entering the ring. There is nothing more embarrassing than a dog shaking and sending up a cloud of dust as the judge is going over him.

When going to the show, try and get to the show site at least two hours before ring time. This will give you and the dog plenty of time to relax, get settled and prepare. If you have extra time, you will have the opportunity to check out the ring for problems such as holes or unexpected mud puddles. You can also watch your judge if he is judging another class and observe his ring procedure, or you can check out the competition. Be an early bird because the pressure will be off. It is the late arrivals who will feel the nerves and get rattled.

Chapter 4
Dress for Success

Proper Ring Attire

Dressing correctly for Junior Showmanship is an important element because it provides the background for the final picture the judge will see. Clothing should be neat, clean and well-pressed. As you graduate from the Junior to Senior division you will notice a drastic change in the dress code. The competition at this level will become more fierce and the wardrobe will reflect this.

Dress Code for Boys

At the very least, you should wear a shirt and tie. Shirts should be clean, pressed and always tucked in. Belts should be worn with slacks with belt loops. A sportcoat, blazer or sweater can be a very nice addition to the shirt and tie. Suits are optional, but you will find when you reach the Open Senior classes they will almost become a must.

Dress Code for Girls

Girls have a wider variety of clothing choices in the Junior Showmanship ring. Dresses, skirts and culottes with sweaters or blouses, and suits with slacks or skirts are all acceptable. Show clothes with pockets are almost a must. With your hands occupied with the show lead, you will need somewhere to store a comb, brush, or bait while in the ring.

Mini-skirts and overly baggy dresses can be distracting and uncomfortable in the ring. A skirt that is too tight can restrict movement. Also, those handlers with small dogs should refrain from wearing long, billowing skirts as they may flap in the dog's face and frighten him or hide him from the judge's view.

Adam Wilkerson demonstrates neat and appropriate attire for boys showing in Junior Showmanship. (Rinehart Photo)

Heather Grodi demonstrates appropriate attire for girls showing in Junior Showmanship. (Photo by K. Booth)

A simple but elegant look will leave a more lasting impression. The key is to be yourself and choose clothing that will complement you and your dog. The most important thing is that you present a neat and professional picture. Clothes do not have to be expensive to look nice.

Color Coordination

Color coordination is important for two reasons. The first, and most obvious, reason is that your clothing colors should match or complement one another. A dark suit with white socks or a brown skirt and dark blue blouse do not coordinate well. Junior Showmanship is not a beauty contest or a fashion show, but a well-coordinated outfit adds to the overall picture you and your dog present.

The second reason for color coordination is not as obvious. Since the handler's position will be behind the dog in the show ring, the clothing color should coordinate with the color of the dog to provide a flattering backdrop for the dog. For example, if you have a dog that is black, you certainly would not wear black clothing because the dog would blend in with your clothing. A light color such as pale blue, white, beige or even red would create a better contrast.

Shoes

Comfortable shoes are a must in the show ring. Shoes with rubber soles are your best bet because their traction is good on any surface. Leather-bottomed shoes will slide like ice skates on slick floor surfaces and wet grass, which could result in an injury to you or your dog. Your shoes should fit well. Losing a shoe while gaiting your dog can disrupt the flow of your performance and distract your dog or those of other exhibitors. Girls should refrain from wearing high heels in the show ring. This type of shoe can be as unstable and as slippery as leather-bottomed shoes. They can also be noisy and frighten your dog during gaiting. Tennis shoes and gym shoes are acceptable. However, large, bulky white Nikes® might not complete the picture you are trying to create with a black suit or a nice dress with nylons.

Hair

For boys or girls, any style is quite acceptable. Hair, like your clothing, should be neat and clean and flatter your appearance. Boys or girls with longer hair might want to consider tying it back in a pony tail. Hair flopping in your face can be quite distracting and uncomfortable when you are trying to stack or gait your dog.

A fashion no-no in juniors.
(Alverson Photo)

Kylie Jo Wolkenheim's black suit serves as a perfect backdrop for her dog and demonstrates the importance of color coordination. (Booth Photo)

Long hair pulled back at outdoor shows can be less distracting for the handler. (Baines Photo)

Neatness Counts

Regardless of what you may hear, neatness does count in the Junior Showmanship and Conformation show ring. Presenting yourself in a neat and clean manner is a sign of respect for the judge and yourself.

Clothes that are pressed, shirts tucked in, shoes tied, and hair in place all are part of the final picture you and your dog present. When you get to the higher levels of Junior Showmanship where competition is tough, a neat appearance may be the little extra that will make the difference between winning and losing.

This photo of Ben Swanson and his Lhasa Apso presents an overall neat appearance and an impressive final picture.(Photo by Steven Ross)

Chapter 5
Basic Training

Types of Show Leads

The show lead can be defined as the source of control, or power, the handler has over the dog. In a literal sense, this means the handler is holding the reins. When chosen wisely, the show lead can lead to triumph. When chosen incorrectly, it can lead to disaster.

Your dog's personality, or any specific problems you are experiencing, will dictate what type of show lead you will use. Each type of lead serves a specific purpose and will correct certain problems.

The most common and widely used leads are the flat and the ribbon leads. The flat leads are for everyday use when your dog does not display any behavioral problems. This lead is wax-coated fabric or synthetic leather that can be stiff. Because of the stiff texture, the coated lead will need to be worked with your fingers to make it more pliable and easier to manipulate. The flat lead measures approximately five and one-half feet in length. This length provides a greater handling comfort for the taller individual. The ribbon leads are approximately a foot and one-half shorter than the flat lead. The lead is named for the woven ribbon-like material (much like canvas) and is more durable for those rough and tumble dogs.

The ribbon leads are available in three different widths: 1/4 inch, 3/8 inch and 5/8 inch. Each width serves a specific purpose. The 1/4 inch lead serves the same purpose as the flat lead, except it is shorter and thinner. The 3/8 inch lead can be used for larger well-behaved breeds or for light corrections on a smaller breed that sniffs the ground occasionally. The 5/8 inch ribbon lead is used for larger dogs. In addition, this lead is used for small to medium-sized breeds that are steeper

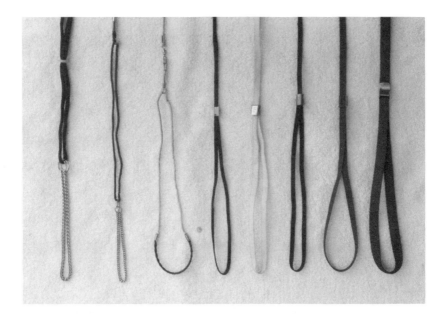

A display of the different type of show leads. From left to right: Heavy Duty Choker; Martingale Choker; Martingale lead; Resco thin lead; Resco thick lead; Simplicity 1/4" lead; Simplicity 3/8" lead; and, Simplicity 5/8" lead.

in shoulder and for persistent ground-sniffing dogs. The added width of the lead creates more pressure on the dog's throat when it is kept taut. This added pressure makes the dog think twice about taking a whiff of the fragrances on the ground.

The swivel, or toy lead, is used for well-behaved small breeds. This lead is no wider than craft floss, but much stronger.

The martingale lead offers more control for handlers with small to medium-sized dogs. The martingale is secured by a swivel ring with a plastic clip rather than the simple, metal slide-clip that fastens the flat and ribbon leads. The most outstanding feature is the attached braided leather collar. This collar and swivel mechanism work much like a choke collar and could be just as effective—but in a more humane fashion. The martingale is also very popular because it is available in dozens of designer colors. The length is approximately five feet.

The martingale choker is made exactly like the martingale lead; however, instead of the braided leather collar, a very fine choke-chain is attached. This lead is available in several different weights. The size you will use will depend on the size and personality of your dog. The martingale choker is used for dogs who are more headstrong and in need of light corrections.

The last lead is the common show-choke collar. This lead is approximately four feet long and constructed of thick cord with a heavy choke chain attached. This lead is used for the larger, more headstrong dog.

I would like to offer a word of advice when using choke or martingale collars. The purpose of these leads is to give the handler more control over the dog. Many times, the choke or martingale leads are used incorrectly. There is a common misconception that dogs who misbehave must be *strung-up* to be corrected. This is untrue. When a dog needs to be corrected, the handler should give the lead a light jerk. The motion should only be enough to gain the dog's attention—not hurt him. A firm "No" should accompany the correction. As long as the dog is behaving there should be no pressure applied to the lead other than to guide him in the direction you wish to gait.

Never use a choke or martingale choke on a dog with a shy or insecure personality. I cannot stress this point enough. One harsh correction on a dog with the wrong personality could ruin an otherwise promising show career. Constant heavy corrections will teach your dog that showing means discomfort.

Placing the Show Lead on Your Dog

The show lead is placed around your dog's neck and secured behind the ears or at the base of the dog's skull (see photo). The show lead should fit tightly enough so the dog cannot wriggle out of it easily, but not too tight. When the lead is secured, you should be able to get at least one finger between the lead and your dog's skin.

Correct Use of the Show Lead

Since the dog will be gaited on your left side, the show lead should be held in the left hand. Once the lead has been placed on your dog and secured, you will need to adjust the length of the lead. The excess lead should be bunched up and hidden in your hand. By leaving the lead dangling from your hand, you not only present an unprofessional picture for the judge, but it can distract your dog as it flaps around.

Regardless of what breed of dog you show, the lead arm should be positioned the same. The arm should be bent at the elbow and should remain stationary (see photo). The reason for keeping your arm in this

Correct positioning of the show lead, front view.

Correct positioning of the show lead, rear view.

position is that you must guide the dog with the lead in that hand. If the hand is constantly moving, so will your dog's head. You will look like a novice handler to the judge. In addition, you will confuse your dog with the excessive movement.

One of my early instructors held a class on the subject of lead-arm positioning. He told us to pretend we were holding a can of pop in our hand and we did not want to spill one drop. He had each of us gait our dogs around the ring with our arms in this position, correcting us if we moved our hands. Many times, we did not realize we were moving our hands or what effect it had upon our dogs' performance. Try practicing this exercise yourself sometime. By perfecting this arm positioning, you will add a great deal to your overall handling picture and your dog will be grateful!

Stacking your Dog

Stacking your dog means to position him in a standing position with both front legs parallel and both back legs parallel. (If you have a German Shepherd, see below.) This facet of showing your dog is as important to your overall performance as gaiting, possibly even more.

Incorrect way to hold show lead. Never let the excess lead dangle.

Correct way to hold show lead. Crumple or fold excess lead in the closed palm of your hand.

Handler with dog shown in stacked position.

Judge going over a junior handler's dog who is in a stacked position.

When you enter the ring, the first impression the judge will have of you and your dog is in the stacked position as he looks over the line for the first time. When you are judged individually, the judge will again see you with your dog in a stacked position. After the judge finishes examining and gaiting the class, he will again look at the group with their dogs in the stacked position. Some judges will make their choices at this time, while others will wait until you have gaited your dog one last time. The judge will see your dog stacked a large percentage of the time and how well you stack your dog could play an important part in where you will place, if at all.

To stack your dog, begin with the front, outside leg. First, allow your dog's head to rest in your right hand. This will give you more control over your dog and will make it easier for you to make a correction if he should move while you are placing him in a stacked position.

With your left hand, grasp the dog's front, outside leg just below the elbow with your index finger resting on the leg. Set the leg down so it is in line with the dog's shoulder. Repeat this step with the right, front leg. Lean back and look to see if the dog's front legs are parallel with each other and the shoulder. It is important to make sure the dog's legs are set under the shoulder, because if they are stacked too far forward or backward it will make the dog's outline look incorrect.

Setting the rear legs is more difficult because every dog is built differently. To set the rear legs, once again start with the outside leg. Hook your thumb and index finger around the back leg just above the hock where it begins to curve. Let your middle finger rest against the back of the leg.

The ideal stacked position of the rear leg is so the hock is positioned straight up and down, or the hock should form a 90-degree angle with the floor. If the foot is placed too far under the dog, the leg will angle downward and look incorrect. If the foot is placed too far back, the pad will be off the floor. With the pad off the floor, the dog could lose traction or break from his stance because he is uncomfortable. Now set the inside back leg in the same manner.

Once you have both legs set in a stacked position, check and make sure the legs are parallel with each other and recheck to make sure the hocks are straight up and down. With a coated breed, it is more difficult to tell if the legs are in the correct position. When I am showing my floor-length-coated Lhasas, I would flatten my hand and turn it palm side in and press it against the hocks to make sure they were parallel and formed a 90-degree angle with the floor. If my hand stayed straight, everything was correct. However, if my hand curved outward or inward, one of the legs was not in position and I would redo the stack.

Once you are satisfied with the way your dog's front and rear are stacked, the positioning of the tail is next. This positioning varies because each breed is constructed a little differently. The following lists are a breakdown of breeds and a description of how the tails should be positioned.

Group A: Afghan Hound, Dalmation, Pointers, Setters, Retrievers, Dachshund, Petit Basset Griffon Vendeen. The tails should be grasped with the thumb, index and middle finger about five inches from the end. The tail should remain level at the base and curve slightly upward at the end.

Group B: Doberman Pinscher, Rottweiler, Spaniels, German Short Hair and Wire Hair Pointers, Viszla, and Weimaraner. The tail should be positioned at a slight angle, not level with the back or straight up in the air. You can hold the tail with the thumb resting under the tail at the end or by holding it with two fingers at the side. Either method is correct and a matter of preference. However, *never grab it like a handle!* You may not have to hold the tail at all as some dogs will hold their tail in this position naturally.

Group C: Beagle, Coonhound, Bloodhound, Foxhound, Harrier, Otterhound, Pharaoh Hound and Ibizan Hound, Poodles, Basset Hound. The tail in this group is held similar to Group A except that the tail is positioned straighter and a little higher in the air. It is better to hold the tail from behind so that your hand does not interfere with the silhouette in the judge's view.

Group D: Bichon Frise, Chows, Tibetan Terrier, Tibetan Spaniel, Lhasa Apso, Shar Pei, Shiba Inu, Finnish Spitz, Basenji, Elkhound, Akita, Malamute, Portuguese Waterdogs, Samoyed, Maltese, Shih Tzu, Pomeranian, Pug, Pekingese, Papillon, Chinese Crested and Chihuahuas. The tail should be held over the back. To keep the tail in position, apply light pressure by using either the palm of your left hand or your thumb and index finger.

Group E: Borzoi, Bullmastiff, Greyhound, Italian Greyhound, Whippet, Wolfhound, Deerhound, Rhodesian Ridgeback, Saluki, Bernese Mountain Dog, Siberian Husky, Newfoundland, Manchester Terrier, Herding Group, Great Dane, Kuvasz, Great Pyrenees, Skye Terrier and Dandy Dinmont Terrier. The tail should remain down resting between the dog's legs.

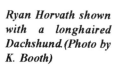

Adam Wilkerson is shown with a Pointer. (Photo by L.F. Sosa)

The following photos are of some of the breeds and their correct positioning for stacking. We have used junior handlers to demonstrate whereever possible; however, we have used photos of adults so that we could represent as many breeds as possible.

Ryan Horvath shown with a longhaired Dachshund. (Photo by K. Booth)

Gary Grossman winning Best Junior Showmanship at the Richmond Kennel Club, 1964. (Photo by Bennett Associates)

Stacy Duncan shown here winning Best Junior Showmanship at Westminster, 1993. (Photo by Chuck and Sandy Tatham)

Anne Olejniczak shown with a Petit Basset Griffon Vendeen.(Booth Photo)

Heather Grodi shown here with a German Shorthaired Pointer.(Baines Photo)

Anne Olejniczak with an English Springer Spaniel. (Ashbey Photo)

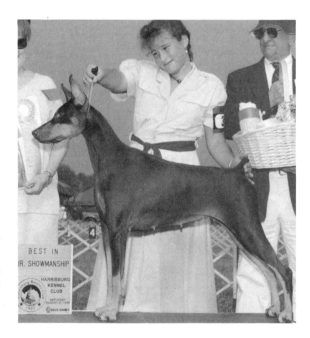

Carissa Demilta is shown here with a Doberman Pinscher. (Ashbey Photo)

Kari Wuornos with a Basset Hound.(Olson Photo)

Camille Lashley with a Toy Poodle.(Photo by Patty Sosa)

Lacey Herbel with a Lhasa Apso. (Callea Photo)

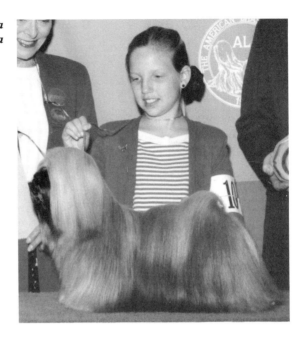

Nancy Allen with a Pekingese. (Photo by Dean Dennis)

Kari Wuornos with an Alaskan Malamute.(Olson Photo)

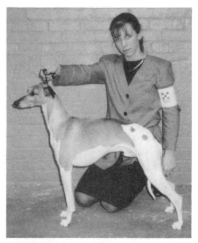

Megan Guthrie with a Whippet.

Colette Livingston with a Portuguese Waterdog.(Photo by K. Booth)

Anne Olejniczak with a Shih Tzu. (Photo by K. Booth)

Melissa Hall with an Australian Shepherd.(Photo by K. Booth)

Adam Wilkerson with a Wirehaired Fox Terrier.

Rex Irwin shown with a Yorkshire Terrier.(Booth Photo)

Theresa Frye and a Cocker Spaniel. (Alex Smith Photo)

Group F: Terriers, Giant and Standard Schnauzer, Silky Terrier, Yorkshire Terrier, Brussels Griffon, and Affenpinscher. Most of these dogs have their tails docked. A light pressure at the tip of the tail applied with your palm or fingertips is all that is necessary.

This outline should answer any basic questions you have about tail positioning. There are no requirements for tail position for Australian Shepherds, Old English Sheepdogs, Schipperke, English Bulldog, French Bulldog and Pembroke Welsh Corgi. If you are in doubt, refer to a book on your breed or ask your dog's breeder for advice.

The final step in stacking your dog is the positioning of the dog's head. Improper positioning of the head is one of the most common stacking mistakes in Junior Showmanship. The dog's neck from the back of the head to the base of the withers should slope into an approximate 60-degree angle. The top of the head should be in a level position parallel with the dog's back. This applies to all breeds except for those that are baited while in a stacked position. The baited dog will be looking upward either at the bait or the handler.

D. Robertson with a German Shepherd. (Photo by Alex Smith)

Now that you know the basics of stacking, the bad news is that the stack must be completed in *10 seconds or less* in the show ring. It will take some time and practice to perfect stacking your dog this quickly, but your experienced competitors will do it this quickly and correctly every time. The judge should never have to wait for you. You should be prepared and waiting for the judge.

Stacking your dog in front of a mirror is a great way to practice. The mirror will show what you and your dog look like from the judge's point of view, and it will also give you an idea of how your dog should look from your angle when he is stacked correctly.

The keys to successful stacking are precision and efficiency. Practice makes perfect, and perfection will make you competitive.

Stacking the German Shepherd

The majority of dog breeds are stacked in a similar manner. A handler may use slight variations with each breed, but the general principle is to stack the dog four square. The exception to this rule is the German Shepherd.

Since I have never shown a German Shepherd, I received information on stacking the German Shepherd from Gail L. Gray, Gene W. Gray and James W. Norris.

To stack the German Shepherd, the handler should start by walking his dog into the posed position. Then while standing in front of his dog, with the collar and chain in the right hand, the handler should pull the dog toward himself until the rear hock of the dog is straight up and down. The leg should now be in a normal stacking position.

After the left foot is positioned, reverse the direction of the pull by gently pushing the dog to stop his forward movement. The inside rear foot should be positioned under the dog. If the leg is not in the correct position, the leg may be placed by hand.

If the front feet are not aligned with the shoulders, then the handler may properly adjust them.

The Grey's and Mr. Norris suggest that the handler always keep one hand under the dog's chin while setting up the front feet. The front legs should be set a palm's width apart, but varies with each dog.

Baiting

When you want to catch a fish, you bait a hook. When showing, you want to catch your dog's attention by showing him bait. You won't use a worm as in fishing unless, of course, your dog has very strange taste in food. In the show ring, you will use bait such as liver, kidneys, chicken or any other food that will draw your dog's attention. Some dogs will not bait for food, but they will bait if you have a

Free baiting a small dog. Please note the position of the handler's hands with the bait.

favorite squeaky toy or stuffed animal. Each dog is an individual, and it will be up to you to find the correct bait.

Learning to use bait correctly is an art. Waving a piece of bait in the air like a flag is not baiting and will not impress anyone in the show ring. Baiting performed properly should be understated—almost like a secret between the dog and handler. A secret that should never be conveyed to the rest of the world.

Bait should be used sparingly while showing the dog in breed or Junior Showmanship. Unlimited access to goodies will not be such a

Free baiting a larger dog.

treat to your dog and his attention will wander. For easy access, bait should be kept in your right pocket while in the ring.

The first rule of baiting is *never throw it in or out of the ring!* Bait littering the ring is an unsightly mess and can become a distraction to other exhibitors' dogs. Many judges have expressed "bait littering their rings" as one of their predominant pet peeves in interviews. So you might want to reconsider throwing your bait in the ring, it may just start you off with one strike against you in the wrong judge's ring! If you find you must throw bait to gain your dog's attention or enhance his expression, be considerate and pick it up afterward.

The second rule of baiting is not to draw attention to yourself by waving bait around as though you were casting a spell. Bait should be held with both hands at waist level when you are standing directly in front of your dog. This form of baiting can also be used when waiting in line and is referred to as *free baiting*.

When baiting your dog, the lead should always be slack. The bait should be held in your right hand with only enough of it showing so the dog knows it is there. If the dog's attention wanes, a quick movement (either downward or to the side) is all you need to do to regain his focus. If he still persists in his inattention, call his name softly during the movement.

Baiting is a test of trust between dog and handler. Some dogs tend to jump up to get the bait. If this happens, a quiet "no" or a light push against the dog with your leg are sufficient corrections.

Working a dog into a self-stacked position.

When you approach the judge after gaiting your dog, position him on the mat in front of the judge. You will then stand off the mat *in the free baiting position* on either side of the judge. Be careful not to come in too close to the judge or position your body in between the judge and your dog. This would prevent the judge from getting a good view of your dog as he is presented in the stacked position.

If you are showing a young, exuberant, inexperienced dog, hold the lead taut, bend slightly and actually allow the dog to chew on the piece of bait in your hand. Make sure you keep most of the bait concealed in your hand so the dog does not snatch the entire piece of bait from your hand all at once. Keep his attention by making ⸱ taste! This form of baiting may not look as appea⸱ to train the inexperienced dog while keeping him⸱

There are two baiting positions you can brin⸱ approaching the judge. You can come straight in an⸱ expression view, which would show off the dog's h⸱ and expression. The other position would give the ju⸱ file view which would accentuate the dog's structure ⸱ ⸱⸱c. These methods are chosen by preference. You might want to ooserve the judge in a previous class as some judges may prefer one view over the other.

There are many variations of baiting. Working handlers will kneel on the floor (in line, of course) and hold a piece of bait in front of the dog's nose. Terrier handlers bend their bodies at the waist and bring the bait to the dog's level. Every handler has a preference and what should be remembered is that the movements should be clean and neat. All styles work, but knowing how to execute them properly is what makes or breaks a performance.

Self-Stacking

When a dog is self-stacked, it means that he has achieved the stacked position without any physical intervention from the handler other than by the use of free-baiting. Baiting and self-stacking go together as Forrest Gump would say, "Like peas and carrots." Without one, you cannot possibly perform the other.

Teaching your dog to self-stack can be a difficult task because some dogs learn new things quickly and others do not. To teach your dog to self-stack, first place him in a stacked position and tell him to "stay." Hold the lead taut and move around all four sides of the dog, holding each position for 10 seconds. Keep repeating the word "stay" in a firm, but not angry, voice. You can begin the self-stacking lessons by moving around your dog on your knees or feet. When you finish the exercise, praise him and give him a piece of bait. Repeat this process several times per day because the only way he will learn is through repetition. Your goal will be to walk around your dog freely when he is in a solid stacked position. Eventually, he will associate self-stacking with food, which will then become free baiting.

Chapter 6
Gaiting

According to Rachel Page Elliott, "The term *gait* means pattern of footsteps at various rates of speed, each pattern distinguished by a particular rhythm and footfall." Gaiting in the show ring is the simultaneous movement of both dog and handler in a prescribed pattern that is designated by the judge. In the conformation ring, the dog is gaited so the judge can evaluate movement in relation to physical structure. Gaiting of the dog in Junior Showmanship allows the judge to evaluate the teamwork between the handler and the dog.

When showing in conformation and Junior Showmanship, the dog is usually gaited at a trot. The speed at which the dog is moved will depend upon the dog's size, structure and balance. At times, the speed may also be determined by the judge. Some judges do not like the dogs moved too quickly in their rings. Other judges may test your skill and knowledge as a handler by requesting that you show your dog at the speed you feel he looks best.

In many instances, the best way to judge the correct speed to gait your dog is to allow him to move at his own pace. Nine times out of ten, the dog will be correct. However, this cannot be the final determining factor. Observing your dog as he is being gaited by someone else is the best method of evaluating his proper pace. Once this pace is determined, you should have someone watch you gait your dog and tell you when the dog has achieved the appropriate pace.

The dog's position at your side while gaiting is crucial. The one thing you *never* want is to have your dog lagging behind you; never drag your dog around the ring. If your dog is a slow mover, tired, or getting bored, you stay in pace with *him*.

Judge gaiting a junior handler and his dog.

Determining the dog's position will depend upon two factors: the dog and the judge. Some dogs, regardless of size, prefer to move out in front of the handler. This position will require the handler to utilize the full length of the lead. If your dog is one of these outgoing individuals, you will have to be sure you have the dog in complete control at all times. With the full length of the lead to play with, an exuberant dog can break stride, visit with an observer at ringside, turn back, or twirl (which could trip you), or break into a run. You could also jeopardize the performance of the junior in front of you if your dog runs into or over his dog. Leave enough room between you and the handler in front to allow for an easy stop or adjustment in speed if the dog in front decides to slow down or comes to a halt.

The second factor regarding your dog's positioning will depend on the judge. There are some judges who do not like the handlers to run in their rings. Never question their motives, just follow their instructions. You might want to observe the judge as he judges one of the classes before you. This way you will know ahead of time if he does not want a fast pace in his ring.

Mats are placed in the ring to provide a solid nonslip surface for your dog to gait on. Therefore, during gaiting the dog should be positioned in the center of the mat. When performing any pattern, it is also important to note that the dog should always be *in a straight line*, unless you are instructed to move in a circle.

Courtesy Turns

"A courtesy turn is a stupid, annoying little circle that gets in your way, and wastes too much time." No, I am only kidding, but when I first entered Open Junior competition, that was my interpretation. In the novice classes (at least when I started), you did not see courtesy turns. We had a difficult enough time with just the basics without trying to perform anything fancy. Because of my inexperience, I did not fully understand the importance of the courtesy turn, and subsequently, brushed it off as a waste of time.

The courtesy turn is a simple and precise 360-degree turn performed with your dog prior to gaiting. Its purpose is to give fluidity to your performance, and if executed correctly, it can be beneficial.

The courtesy turn is like a warm up before you start a pattern. It awakens your dog and signals that it is time to get started. All you need to do is gait your dog in a small circle in front of the judge. Make sure you leave enough room so the circle is not performed "on top of the judge." The turn should be small, controlled, and smooth so that it flows into the pattern.

Courtesy turns are used before you begin your pattern and again before heading to the end of the line. You can also use a courtesy turn when doing the triangle as you prepare to gait your dog down the

Entering the courtesy turn.

Dog gaits around the handler.

Dog continues to gait around the handler.

Finishing the courtesy turn.

diagonal and approach the judge. The courtesy turn can be awkward for handlers with smaller dogs, such as the Yorkshire Terrier or Dachshund. Because of their size, small dogs can be hidden behind their handlers during the turn. On the other hand, the larger dogs benefit from this move since it assists in keeping fluidity to their gait during patterns.

The courtesy turn in Junior Showmanship is optional. When executed correctly, it can add that something extra to your performance. Consequently, if it is clean and smooth, your performance will leave a good impression and may increase your chances for success.

I must offer you a word of warning about using courtesy turns in Junior Showmanship. Some judges will ask you not to do any of the "tricks" at the beginning of the class. In most cases, this is in reference to the turns. So make sure that you *always* follow the judge's instructions.

Switching Hands.

Step one.   *Step two.*

Switching Hands

One of the most important rules of Junior Showmanship is *never let anything get between your dog and the judge*. This includes you! To prevent this from happening, you will have to learn to switch the lead from one hand to the other and gait the dog on the opposite side. This process is called "switching hands." The decision on when and where to

Step three.

Step four.

switch hands will depend on the pattern you are performing and the position of the judge.

One of my early instructors demonstrated a very simple way to switch hands. When you get to the end of the mat and are ready to turn, clap your hands together and grasp the lead in the opposite hand. This method of switching hands will seem quite primitive at first. However, with practice, the motion will become more fluid and the judge will barely notice you have made the transfer.

Gaiting Patterns

Junior Showmanship evolved extensively during the eight years I was eligible to show. When I retired, the variety of patterns requested by judges had been greatly reduced. However, knowing all of the patterns proved to be of invaluable assistance. Not only was practicing the various patterns a good lesson in discipline, but it also prepared me for those judges who did decide to request something other than the usual patterns. Success in Junior Showmanship means always being prepared.

The Down and Back

The most widely used pattern in conformation and Junior Show-manship is the down and back. The down and back can be performed either on the diagonal mat or on one of the side mats. On occasion, a

The Ring

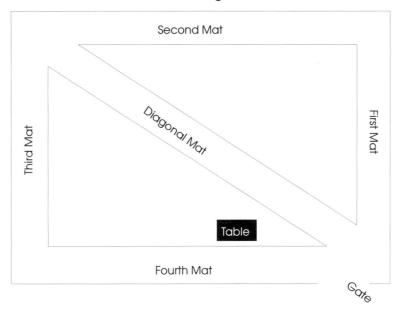

The Down and Back

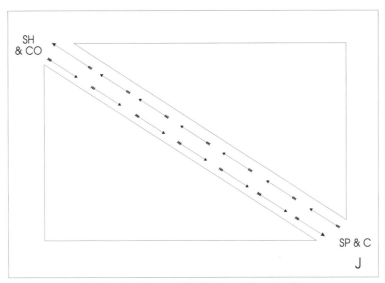

Cı Courtesy Turn   COı Optional Courtesy Turn
Jı Judge   SHı Switch Hands   SP: Starting Point

judge will ask you to move across the ring in a down and back pattern while you are in line where there are no mats. In the description of each pattern in this chapter, I will make reference to the points in each where a courtesy turn will be performed. If you have decided not to use courtesy turns when showing in Junior Showmanship, disregard the reference points and follow the pattern as stated.

To perform the down and back, you begin by doing a courtesy turn in front of the judge. Move the dog down the mat in a straight line away from the judge. The dog should be gaited to the end of the mat to the point where the mats come together. Perform a courtesy turn quickly, check the judge's position and bring your dog back again, stopping approximately two feet from the judge. Make sure you pay close attention to the judge on the return because he may request that you stop sooner than the two feet I have mentioned.

In larger rings, or if you have a smaller dog, the judge may ask you to go halfway down and back. Be sure that you pay strict attention to his instructions.

A deviation from the usual down and back pattern may happen when you are stacked in line as a group. As the judge is making his final determination, he may have you move your dog down and back from your position in line. In this situation, pay close attention to the judge's instructions. He may ask you to take "six steps and come back," or to "go halfway down and back." Most of these occurrences will take place off the standard mat path. All you can do is take your time, move in as straight a line as possible and to the judge's specifications.

Before the change in Junior Showmanship rules in 1989, the judges used to move their positions in the ring. The purpose of this change in position was to see if you were paying attention to position during gaiting. This change in position often required the junior handler to switch hands on the down and back rather than doing a courtesy turn. You will rarely run into this situation; usually it will happen under judges who have been judging Junior Showmanship for a long time before the rule changes.

The "L"

The "L" is the most difficult pattern to do. It can be tricky, but once you learn it, the other patterns will be much easier to perform. The "L" usually will start on the first mat, which is the one closest to the ring entrance. The construction of this pattern is self-explanatory, but what sets it apart from the down and back is that you will have to switch hands in two places on the return.

The "L"

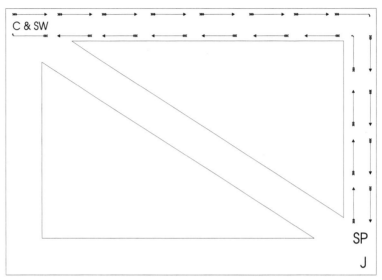

C: Courtesy Turn   J: Judge
SH: Switch Hands   SP: Starting Point

The "L" (optional variation due to judge's position)

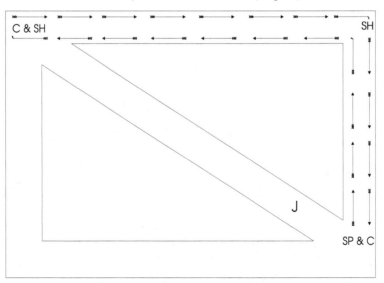

C: Courtesy Turn   J: Judge
SH: Switch Hands   SP: Starting Point

You will begin the "L" with the dog gaiting on your left side on the first and second mats. When you reach the end of the second mat, where the diagonal meets, you will switch hands and make a 180 degree turn. You will now be moving in the opposite direction heading back toward the judge. The dog will be gaiting on your right side so that your body does not get between the judge and your dog. When you reach the first mat, switch hands once again and cross the dog in front of you so that the dog is once again on your left hand side. You will then approach the judge in the same manner as in the down and back.

In the Open classes of Junior Showmanship, flair becomes a factor. When switching hands during the "L," you may perform a courtesy turn each time to make the transition look cleaner. This decision is entirely up to you, and I must stress that you should not try to perform anything fancy until you are ready. Practice at home first to make sure you understand the process. There is nothing more embarrassing than going to a show, trying to pull off a brilliant move and having it backfire. This happened to me the year before I retired from Junior Showmanship when I was breaking in a new dog. I was experienced and confident, but my dog had other ideas!

The Triangle

Like the "L," the triangle starts on the first mat and continues to the second. At the intersection of the second mat and diagonal mat, you will turn and bring your dog down the mat to the judge. You will again approach the judge as you did in the down and back.

There are three variations you may use when turning the corners in the triangle. The first variation is what is known as the simple or training method which has been described above.

The second variation is called the traditional method. This method incorporates the courtesy turn in the corner before coming down the diagonal. When performed correctly, the traditional method gives a nice transition and easily aligns you with the judge as you approach. This is the most commonly used method.

The third method is the one I used most often. It requires the dog to do the courtesy turn in the corner before coming down the diagonal. The third method is much flashier than the simple method and a much cleaner transition than the traditional. Many judges took note of this turn because it was different and creative. However, as with any new addition to your handling techniques, you must practice extensively before trying it in the ring.

The Triangle

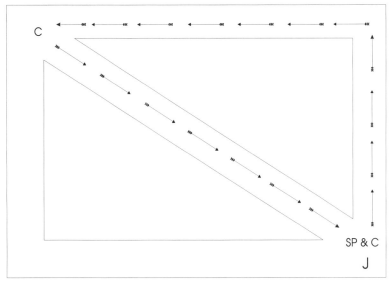

C: Courtesy Turn   J: Judge   SP: Starting Point

Taking Your Dog to the End of the Line

Although this may not be considered a traditional pattern, you will take your dog to the end of the line after examination every time you show him in the breed classes or Junior Showmanship. Many times, the judge will watch as you gait to the end of the line. In the breed classes, he may do this because he was impressed with the conformation or movement of your dog and wishes to evaluate further. In Junior Showmanship, he may be impressed with your skills as a handler and may be comparing you to others who have preceded you in line. The important thing is that you want to leave a good, lasting impression as you take your dog to the end of the line.

When observing the Junior Showmanship classes, you can always differentiate between the veteran junior handlers and the newcomers. Junior handlers of lesser experience will take the dog to the end of the line and simply restack their dogs. This is not the best thing to do because it is time consuming.

The veterans will always take note of the judge to see if he is watching as they take their dogs to the end of the line. If the judge is watching, they will use it to their advantage. The veteran handlers will take their dogs to the end of the line and begin to slow their dogs a few feet from where they wish to stop. They will turn their bodies so they are facing their dogs and walk the dogs into a free-baited stacked position. This is a clean, no-fuss way to end the pattern, unless your dog decides not to cooperate.

If your dog does not cooperate, do not give up even if the judge has turned away. Keep at it until you get it right. My dad once told me while we were shooting baskets in the front yard never to quit at a low point. And, always sink the ball one last time and finish strong. This advice can be applied to an uncooperative dog. Do it until it is right.

You can also apply this free-baiting method while you are waiting in line. Whenever the judge chooses to look over the line, your dog will be under control and presenting a complimentary picture. This method will work regardless of the size of your dog or whether the breed is supposed to be free baited or not. Constantly forcing the dog into a stacked position for long periods of time is tedious and boring. Free-baiting is a more relaxing and enjoyable way for both you and your dog to spend your time waiting.

The Reverse Triangle, Angle "L" and the "T"

The reverse triangle, angle "L" and "T" are complex patterns that are rarely used. The reason I have put these patterns in this chapter is that judges did request them during my Junior Showmanship years. In addition to the usual patterns, my practice routine at home always included the reverse triangle, angle "L" and "T." Because my dog and I were familiar with these patterns, my performance was not affected by the judges' unusual request. As I have mentioned, success in Junior Showmanship means always being prepared.

The reverse triangle and the angle "L" combine the elements of the triangle and the "L." One requires just switching hands, the other involves both switching hands and a courtesy turn.

Now that you understand the triangle and the "L," you should understand these two patterns quite easily. Practice will be necessary to perform this pattern in a smooth, clean manner.

In the reverse triangle, you will begin gaiting the dog on your left side on the diagonal away from the judge. You will go down the diagonal to the second mat. Rather than turning left and proceeding to the end of the line, you will go to the right. You will gait on this mat exactly like the second half of the "L." As you get to the corner where the diagonal

The Reverse Triangle

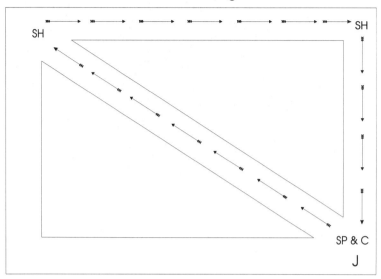

C: Courtesy Turn   J: Judge
SH: Switch Hands   SP: Starting Point

The Angle "L"

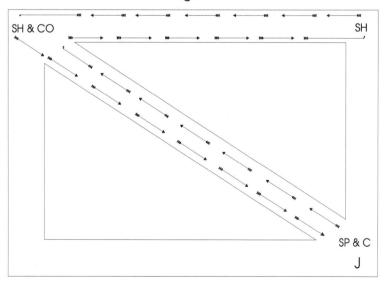

C: Courtesy Turn   CO: Optional Courtesy Turn
J: Judge   SH: Switch Hands   SP: Starting Point

The "T"

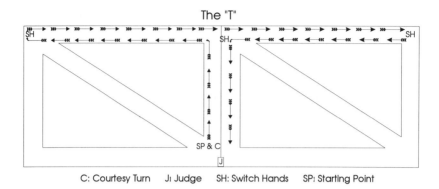

C: Courtesy Turn   J: Judge   SH: Switch Hands   SP: Starting Point

and second mat meet, you will turn on the corner behind your dog and switch hands. This will prevent you from hiding your dog from the judge's view. You will then finish the pattern as you did in the traditional form of the "L."

I have only encountered the angle "L" one time toward the end of my Junior Showmanship career. The judge was having difficulties making his decision in a large Open Senior class; so he had each junior perform a different pattern.

The angle "L" also begins on the diagonal. You will be required to switch hands as you did with the reverse as you transfer onto the second mat. You will then proceed to the first mat and switch hands. Instead of finishing by gaiting your dog down the first mat, you will make a 180 degree turn and go back down the second mat. When you reach the diagonal you will finish the pattern as in the traditional form of the triangle.

I have saved the most unusual pattern for last which is the "T." If you are asked to perform this pattern, it will most likely be in a ring with no mats, (or if you show in the group ring), or at an outdoor show.

When you look at the "T," you would think you could begin on either side of the dog. However, you cannot. You must start with the side where the dog faces the judge, which will usually be the left side. To begin the "T," gait your dog straight away from the judge. As you reach the end of the straightaway, you will turn left. If there are no mats, you will travel about the same distance as you did on the straightaway. When you reach this distance, you will make a 180 degree turn and switch hands, so your dog remains in full view of the judge. You will gait your dog past the straightaway and proceed the same approximate distance from that point as you did on the other side. You will again switch hands and gait your dog back to the intersection with the straightaway. At the intersection, you will bring the dog down the straightaway back to the judge. You will not need to change hands at the intersection, unless the judge has moved and is on your right side.

The Procedure when Gaiting Against Another Dog

When the rules for Junior Showmanship were changed in 1989, the judges were discouraged from gaiting two dogs together side by side. However, I had several judges who requested this pattern in Junior Showmanship despite the discouragement by AKC. Therefore, I am including it in this chapter so you can familiarize yourself with the procedure if you are ever asked to perform it.

The key to performing this pattern correctly is for you, the handler, not to be positioned between the two dogs during gaiting. In conformation, this pattern is requested so the judge can compare the movement of the two dogs by moving them side by side. In Junior Showmanship, the handling skill of the Junior is being tested. If you are caught in the middle of two dogs, you will impair the judge's view.

If you are lucky enough to be designated to the right side of the pair by the judge, you will begin gaiting your dog away from the judge with the dog on your left side. When you make the turn to return to the judge, you will switch hands and remain on the same side of the dog and finish the pattern as you would in the down and back.

If you are designated to the left side, your handling skills will be greatly tested. You will begin gaiting your dog away from the judge with the dog on your right side. When you make the turn to return to the judge, you will switch hands and remain on the same side of the dog and finish the pattern as you would in the down and back.

This pattern is not about staying on the outside and switching hands, but more importantly about working with someone else. Before you begin to gait this pattern, make sure that the other handler is ready. This is not a foot race. You should try to match the other dog, stride for stride, so that they look like mirror images during the pattern.

Chapter 7
The Finer Points

Once you have learned the basic techniques of handling and have graduated to the finer points, it will be time to start thinking about developing your own style of handling. Each person is an individual, and in the show ring it is necessary to *show* as an individual. If your handling technique mimics 16 other juniors in your class, you will decrease your chances of winning. The judge can only choose one winner, and if the entire class consists of little "handling clones," his choice will probably be a toss-up. To avoid falling into this category, it will be necessary for you to establish your own style of handling.

Showing dogs is a creative and artistic sport. The medium used to create this artistry will be your hands and body language. Your handling skills will enhance your dog's good features and camouflage his flaws so that the completed picture will be a work of art.

Before developing your own style, study the styles of the better professional and junior handlers. These observations can spark your imagination, which is where your creating will begin. Do not copy another's style, but try to incorporate some of the more impressive moves, or a variation of your own making, into your handling routine. You will be, I hope, far enough advanced in your show career that you will be able to differentiate between correct and incorrect handling techniques. The last thing you want to do is mimic another person's bad habits!

Creating your own style of handling will help you grow as a handler. The key to winning consistently in Junior Showmanship is through constant work to improve your skills. You are never too old, or too experienced, to learn something new. Establishing your own style can give you that something extra needed to be successful—like the winning edge.

Practice, Practice, Practice

Carl Lewis did not run the 100 meter sprint in 9.86 seconds on his first try. It took many years of practice and dedication to become the fastest man alive. The same can be said about dog handling. Showing is a sport, but handling is an art. Your ring presence should be one of grace, poise and confidence. Although it is not a beauty contest, handling requires related skills. The only way to develop these skills is by intense practice requiring self-discipline. Although there may be many days when you do not feel like practicing, it will be worth the effort to push yourself. You won't regret it when you get into the show ring.

Your practice sessions need not be as long as a training class. A 10-minute routine once a day is all it takes. To teach your dog and yourself discipline, all you have to do is go through all the patterns—the triangle and its reverse, the "L," the "T," the angle "L" and the down and back. Many of the patterns are not used that often, but it is best to know them well. I exhibited at a show once in which the judge asked for a reverse triangle. Many of the juniors were confused because they had never heard of this pattern. For months my Lhasa and I had been practicing the reverse triangle and the "T" (which the judge later called for in Best Junior Handler). The endless days of practicing those same old boring patterns became worthwhile after all. I gained a victory from learning them.

With regular practice sessions, your performance will flow more easily into each step without any stops or breaks, and your dog will learn to maintain a steady gait. Smoothness is a handling characteristic highly regarded by judges. It provides the impression of ultimate teamwork which will be discussed below.

Your practice sessions need not be like boot camp. All you need is a few minutes to run through the patterns and work on minor flaws. By doing this you will find your performances will improve, and you too can become a challenging force.

Becoming a Team with Your Dog

Think of showing as a team sport—a team of two, you and your dog. A team is built on friendship, trust and precision. Your goal is to get 100 percent out of your partner. If you give, your dog will give. The key to winning as a team is in your dog's response to your commands.

The teamwork between a dog and the handler can begin at a very young age.

If you and your dog are working on two different wavelengths, you are going to lose.

A good example of teamwork is the sport of dressage. In the *Encyclopedia of the Horse*, dressage is defined as "the art of training horses to perform all movements in a balanced, supple, obedient and keen manner." This does not mean that your dog has to behave like a little soldier, because it won't happen. A dog is a living, breathing creature much like ourselves, but of the four-legged variety. He has a mind of his own and feelings.

Some days your dog will have his own ideas on how things should be done. That is when your handling capabilities will be tested. If you get flustered and angry at the dog, it will reveal to the judge your inexperience. You may get angry with your dog, but learn to control your feelings. When your dog acts up, handle him in a calm and cool manner. I had many wins that I thought were losses because my dog was not cooperating; however, I never gave up trying to make my dog behave. I kept things under control, and the judges recognized that fact. Junior Showmanship is supposed to be judged on how you handle—not how your dog shows, which is the purpose of conformation.

Returning to the dressage concept, dressage combines skill and grace with strength and discipline. This perfectly sums up what handling is all about. Just like a dressage rider, you and your dog should give the impression of "elegance and complete harmony, with rhythmical movements and precision timing." Think of your dog's lead as a horse's rein leading to a bit. Your signals should be light in hand so that your dog displays movements with no physical effort. Dressage at its highest level is pure poetry in motion, with horse and rider working together as one, a feat that is not easily accomplished.

For you and your dog to attain this goal, spend extra time with him in addition to your 10-minute practice sessions. Teamwork is not only obtained through practice, but also through friendship. Don't just be your dog's master—be his friend. When you are relaxing in the evening, let your dog watch television with you. Take him for a romp around the property or neighborhood. Or, just take some time out and play with your dog. Let's face it, the average show dog does not get special privileges such as those mentioned above. A little extra TLC will get you where you want to go—and further.

Be Alert at Ringside

Many exhibitors take their dog's safety at ringside for granted. However, at times so many dogs and handlers are crammed into a small, enclosed area that in the confusion unnecessary accidents can take place. Many things can occur outside the ring. Dogs can be stepped on, have drinks dumped on them, be burned by a cigarette, etc. The dangers could be compared to those encountered when walking down a darkened alley alone at night. There is always the notion that someone or something is lurking in the shadows, and remaining alert is the key to survival.

There are many ignorant and careless exhibitors at dog shows who do not keep their dogs under control at all times. Therefore, you must learn to handle your dog defensively at ringside. Chad, a Lhasa Apso, was one of my first Junior Showmanship dogs. While we were waiting at ringside for my class, he was unexpectedly attacked by an Akita, whose owner was busy talking with friends. The Akita's lead had slackened to the point where he had enough room to get to my dog—just four feet away. The attack was so intense that the Akita's mouth had to be pried from my dog's neck. Fortunately, Chad had a thick coat, so the other dog had gotten mostly hair in his mouth, and Chad was uninjured. Directly after this incident, my class was called into the ring. Chad showed like a trooper and suffered no ill effects from this incident, other than being wary of large dogs at ringside from that day forward. I was lucky. Chad was a very confident dog; however, many dogs would have been so stressed by the incident that they would never have shown again.

The situation with Chad could have been avoided if the Akita's owner had been more responsible. However, it is your responsibility to take proper care of your dog at ringside. As this situation illustrates, you cannot always depend on other people's good judgment. To keep your dog out of harm's way at ringside, always place him away from the confusion. Positioning your dog right behind the ring fencing is always a safe place to stand or kneel with him. The fencing protects one side, and you can protect the other. This way if there is any potential danger at ringside, your dog is secure.

Just remember that dark alley. There is always some unknown force waiting to test your alertness. Stay on your toes for the sake of your dog.

Never Let Anything Get Between Your Dog and the Judge

When actors perform on stage, they must be certain the audience can see them at all times. Their backs should never be to the audience, and the props should not block anyone's view, even their own. The same principle may be applied to the Junior Showmanship ring. The judge is the audience, you and your dog are the actors, and the show ring the stage. Judges should never see your back in the ring, except when you are gaiting your dog away from them.

The first commandment of Junior Showmanship is **never** let anything or anyone get between the judge and your dog. While the dogs are stacked in line, you should be prepared to move around your dog if the judge moves into a position in which his view of your dog would be

obstructed. If you are stacking a small dog on the floor and you are on your knees, you may have to move around the dog on your knees. Handlers with larger dogs will be able to step around their dogs quite easily. It can be very advantageous for a junior with a smaller dog to move around his dog while he is in a standing position. The junior's movements will look smoother to the judge, and it will be less painful for the handler's knees, especially at indoor shows with ribbed floor mats. Practice with your dog, and teach him to stand still while performing this maneuver before using it in the ring. The benefits will be worth the effort.

Many veteran Junior Showmanship judges like to weave between each exhibitor and dog while they are stacked in line to see if the handlers are paying attention. This is where novice competitors make their most common mistakes. Often they remain in position behind the dogs, when it would be better to move to the side or front of the dogs to ensure they are not blocking the judge's view.

Another common error occurs when the judge requests that all dogs be stacked with their fronts or rears facing him. Some handlers will find themselves on the judge's side of the dogs, hence getting between the judge and their dogs. The best way to avoid blocking the judge's view is to stand behind your dog when stacking the front or in front of your dog when stacking the rear. As this may not be applicable for all dogs, your alternative is to make sure you are **always** on the opposite side of the dog the judge is viewing. You can also apply these maneuvers when the judge is moving around your dog.

Another point you should be aware of is gaiting and the judge's position. When you approach the judge after executing a pattern, be prepared to move around the dog while he is self-stacked in front of the judge so you do not obstruct the judge's vision of your dog.

When judging difficult classes, Junior Showmanship judges are constantly checking to see if you are alert. Don't let them catch you off guard; it could cost you a win or a placing.

Just as actors on stage use props, you use props such as the table in the show ring. When the show is indoors, the table can be a nuisance. There is no way to avoid going behind the table without risking your dog's footing. The floors at most indoor shows are very slippery, which is why the club provides mats in the ring. When you leave the mat, your dog's feet may slip and slide, thus breaking the flow of his gait and subjecting him to conditions that could result in an injury. There are products, such as Tacky Paw®, that can be applied to your dog's pads before showing to give him better traction on slippery surfaces. These products are helpful, especially if your dog has a tendency to cut corners when gaiting. However, even with this type of insurance, there is always a chance your dog's feet will slip.

When stacking your dog, make sure you never do so behind the table; otherwise, the judge's view is blocked. This is a very common mistake among *all junior handlers*, not just the novice competitors.

When exhibiting at outdoor shows, the same rule applies. However, since there are no mats, and the surface your dog is moving on has solid footing, it is acceptable to move in front, rather than behind, the table. This can be applied to your individual gaiting pattern, as well as gaiting with the group.

Outdoor shows present another possible obstruction to deal with—the poles that hold up the tents. When stacking, you have two options unless the judge gives you definite instructions. The first is to go between the poles, lining up parallel to them and stacking your dog; or, just move a few feet in front of them and stack your dog. Either alternative is acceptable and is subject to your own preference.

The same rules that apply to moving around the table can be applied to the poles. Many juniors make the mistake of going under the tent when gaiting their dogs. You **should avoid doing this.** Since gaiting thus will not only place your dog behind the many poles, but will also hide your dog in the shade. If the line is headed for under the tent, wait until the other handlers clear out from under it (to ensure you don't accidentally cut someone off) and then cut in front of the poles. By doing this you give the judge the impression you are experienced, alert and under control.

In Junior Showmanship, it is important always to be aware of the judge's location, and that your dog is always within his view. This is the purpose for switching hands during the patterns and moving around the table or tent poles. Small details can make a difference between winning and losing, so remember how critical your audience can be and always put on a good performance.

The Blind Courtesy Turn

When I showed my Lhasa Apsos in Junior Showmanship and the breed classes, I discovered a "blind courtesy turn" was impressive. By "blind," I mean that you and your dog are going to move in two different directions. To utilize this turn effectively, complete trust is essential between the dog and the handler. In a traditional courtesy turn, both the dog and the handler participate, but in the blind courtesy turn only

THE BLIND COURTESY TURN.

Step one.

Step two.

Step three.

Step four.

Step five.

the dog pivots. He remains on your left side; however, he does the turn in front of you and always remains in plain view of the judge. This move could be compared to swinging a dance partner during the tango.

As with anything, there is a flip side to this impressive move. If your dog does not know it well enough, or decides he does not want to do it, you are in trouble. This is a mistake that is difficult to cover up. Therefore, it is important that you drill and drill your dog so that it becomes an automatic or an almost unconscious movement.

The blind courtesy turn is much like the second turn on the comeback of the "L," except that your dog goes in the other direction. Many times it proved to be beneficial in Junior Showmanship when I chose to use the blind courtesy turn with one of my Lhasa Apsos. A number of judges were very impressed with that silly little turn.

You will find that the blind courtesy turn can be applied to the down and back as well. You can also use it on the comeback of the "T," although it is only on rare occasions that you will be asked to do a "T."

Watching the Judge

You should avoid allowing something or someone to get between your dog and the judge. It is important, therefore, to always know where the judge's position is in the show ring. Your peripheral vision (looking from the side of your eye) is the fundamental skill used in this technique, and subtlety is essential.

The technique will be especially beneficial when you are doing your individual patterns. When moving with the group, you should glance at the judge every so often so that you are aware of the judge's location. The only time you look directly at the judge is when you are in a blind spot. Your blind spots are:

A) the turn onto the diagonal mat on the comeback of the triangle;

B) the turn off the diagonal on the reverse triangle;

C) the turn around on the first leg of the down and back.

In these key areas you should always check for the judge's position as many will move just to see if you are paying attention. When watching the judge, be sure your glance is quick. In time, it should become an unconscious movement that just flows with your routine. The rest of the time you should use your peripheral vision.

There are three reasons for using a quick glance when watching the judge. First, a quick glance will not be mistaken for staring, which can be irritating to the judge. Second, the quick glance allows you to concentrate on your dog and where you are going, and still be conscious of the judge's position. I have observed many Juniors over the years who never took their eyes off the judge during the entire class. They looked like gawkers at the scene of an accident. While they were focusing all of their attention on the judge, their dogs could have been rolling on the floor on their backs, or could have restacked themselves with toplines of swaybacked horses. The third reason is that it looks better. Instead of gaping at the judge every two steps, you subtly check his location.

When the dogs are stacked at the beginning of your class and the judge first looks over the line, you should look up at the judge as he looks at you and your dog. It is a standard procedure, almost like a greeting, and an acknowledgment showing the judge that you are alert.

There is another method of judge watching known as "the stare down." This is used during the crucial moment when the judge is ready to make the final decisions. You look at the judge with confidence as if to say, "Here I am. I did a good job. Put me up!" It is a common practice of many professional handlers, and it can be a form of intimidation. You must be careful, however, never to use this technique as intimidation yourself, as instead of intimidating the judge you may well provide a reason to dislike your performance.

Smoothing the hand along the dog's neck and topline accentuates those qualities.

Watching the judge is an aspect of Junior Showmanship that requires good judgment. It can be especially useful if it seems the judge is having a difficult time making a decision, and it could be the boost you need to earn a win. So use, but don't abuse, the purpose of watching the judge.

Showing off the Dog's Good Points

Regardless of what breed you show, the method of drawing attention to your dog's good points can be applied universally. Prior to entering the realm of sporting dogs, I exhibited Lhasa Apsos for eight years. Acquiring Cricket, an English Springer Spaniel, proved to be the turning point in my Junior Showmanship and Conformation career. She expanded my knowledge of basic handling techniques, which later helped me.

To gain an understanding of what I mean, you must first step into the world of sporting dogs. Take time out at a show and watch some of the better sporting handlers in the breed and group ring. The skills they employ to extract the best performance possible from their dogs and enhance their strong points are many. They truly are the artists of the handling world.

FRAMING THE DOG'S HEAD.

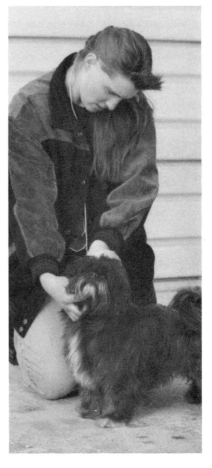

Every dog, regardless of breed, has strengths and weaknesses. The job of a good handler is to maximize his dog's good points and minimize the weak ones. For example, Cricket has a beautiful spaniel head, which is correct by the breed standard. She also has an excellent front assembly with good shoulders and chest, and straight forelegs. To accentuate all of these qualities, I would stack her at a slight angle, with her front legs pointed slightly out, toward the judge. This small deviation from the normal stacking position allowed the judge a good view of Cricket's strong points at first glance. To add extra emphasis, when he was looking at her, I would run two fingers across the top of her head and from her withers to the base of her tail. Light movements used to accentuate your dog's good points are referred to as "finger works" and are used only when you are stacking your dog.

"Finger works" are most commonly applied to the head, neck, withers and topline. They are simple, but effective movements that can accentuate these areas with one simple brush of the hand. To show off the head using finger works, all that is necessary is to run two fingers across the top of the dog's skull, and then look back up at the judge. To create extra emphasis, you can frame the head as well. Framing is

This junior pulls her dog out further from the rest to accentuate the fact that her dog has a good front.

the process of holding the dog's head in your right hand and resting two fingers from the left hand behind the ears.

You can show off the wither and topline by running two fingers from the top of the wither to the base of the tail. Again, once you have completed the move, be sure to look back up at the judge.

Over the years, I have observed some handlers accenting the front or rear of their dogs by running their fingers down those areas. This move is rarely used because the areas can be so large they could require the entire arm to point them out—quite time consuming.

A few years ago while showing in Junior Showmanship, I discovered there was a way to accentuate my dog's movement. The dog I was showing at the time, Michael, was a Lhasa Apso with exceptional movement. Although he was a small breed, he proved to be a great dog for Junior Showmanship because he could move as swiftly as an Afghan Hound or a Golden Retriever. On this particular day, the judge was nearly ready to make her decision on the placements in the class. She asked each of us to "show off" our dog's best feature. I failed to place that day; so I later asked her why. *She told me that I never looked at the dog and then at her, to reinforce the fact that the dog had good movement.* A simple, but costly mistake.

Finger works, framing, and reinforcing glances can all emphasize your dog's good points. Mastering these skills will not only help you in the Junior Showmanship ring, but in the breed ring when you begin competing with the big kids.

Be Quick and Accurate about Restacking

You are in the show ring, and the judge is going over your dog. He lifts your dog's rear leg and moves it out of position. You have only one response. You fix it as quickly and accurately as possible.

Simple dilemmas, such as this, can tarnish an otherwise adept performance in the Junior Showmanship ring, especially when you have reached the more competitive Open Senior class or Best Junior Handler. When competing with the best, minor flaws can create a loss.

The process of stacking should only take about 10 seconds. Restacking could take as little as one second if your dog has only moved one leg; however, it could take considerably longer if your dog is fidgeting or if he has completely broken from his stance. These are good reasons for practicing stacking and restacking as much as possible. Practice is important.

The best way to teach yourself to be quick and accurate is to play dog show with your dog. Find a space outside, or in your home, that you can use as a mock show ring. Practice stacking your dog, then relaxing with him for a few minutes, and repeat the entire exercise once again. Once you feel you have mastered the stacking process, kidnap a family member or friend to play judge. Ask the judge to go over your dog and move a leg or two out of position. Then practice restacking. If you are really conscientious, you can even use a stopwatch to time your progress.

The only way to attain the goal of quickness and accuracy while restacking is through repetition. Just remember, a judge is not going to wait all day for you to neaten up your dog. Make his day, and yours, a great deal better by being quick and accurate.

Always Gait Your Dog at His Normal Speed
There are more than 130 breeds of dogs recognized by the American Kennel Club, and these breeds come in different shapes and sizes. Regardless of your breed—Yorkshire Terrier, Shih Tzu, Welsh Corgi, Lakeland Terrier, Cocker Spaniel, German Shepherd or Great Dane— all dogs are individuals. Each dog, even within his own breed, has a pace (when gaiting) that looks best. Your job, as a handler, is to determine this speed and maintain it when showing the dog.

If you are a beginner, or even a seasoned veteran, you may need assistance in establishing your dog's best pace. Ask your parents, a friend, or handling instructor to watch you gait your dog and let you know at what speed he shows to advantage. If you wish to determine this yourself, you might have someone video tape while you are gaiting your dog. If you do not have a video camera, try gaiting by a series of glass windows that will project the actions while you are gaiting your dog. This can also give you some idea of how you and your dog look from the judge's point of view.

Many juniors make the mistake of forcing their dogs to move too fast in an attempt to keep up with the rest of the class. This results in either the dog being dragged behind you or breaking from a trot into a gallop. Neither alternative will make an appealing picture for the judge. If your dog is smaller, do not be intimidated by the speed of the larger breeds. When showing with the group, or on your individual pattern, don't rush the dog's performance. The best handlers never do, whether it is in Junior Showmanship, the breed classes, group or Best in Show.

If your dog is a larger variety, and you find yourself behind a dog that moves more slowly, hold your dog back. Allow enough space so you can bring your dog to his best pace as you reach the judge's view.

This enables you to show your dog at a smooth, steady gait when it is most important, and it prevents you from running up and possibly spooking the dog in front of you.

Keep in mind, the rules for Junior Showmanship state clearly that the dog is to be shown in the same manner as in the breed ring. Consequently, gaiting your dog should not mimic the Indy 500 or a snail's pace. Be individualistic and always gait your dog at his best pace.

Relax in the Ring with Your Dog

Showing dogs is a fast-paced, tension-filled sport that requires a great deal of concentration. It is easy at times to get caught up in the winning aspect of the sport, and the consequences can become quite apparent in the show ring. It is natural for you to want your dog to look his best at all times, and that is when a major mistake is made by many junior handlers. When they get in the ring, all they do is stack their dogs, wait for their turns, and after their turns, they go right back to stacking their dogs. Not only is this extremely boring, but it creates more tension for you and your dog.

Rather than stacking and restacking your dog the entire time in the ring, relax with him instead. There are many ways this can be accomplished. If it is a large class, let your dog lie down and sit down beside him, or if your dog has a favorite toy, bring it in the ring and play with

Angling the dog on the mat while self-stacking.

him. When the judge has progressed down the line to two juniors in front of you, begin preparing your dog for examination or gaiting.

Since dogs, like people, have different personalities, it may not be easy to get your dog to relax or play with a toy in the ring. My Lhasas were usually too dignified to play with a toy, and my Springer was very hyper and never stood still for any length of time. The form of relaxation that worked best with my dogs was free baiting. It is a simple, but profitable, procedure. For one thing, your dog enjoys the food reward, and because of the reward you have his undivided attention which in turn will relax you both. It also keeps your dog constantly under control without boring him, and if the judge should glance down the line during the class, your dog is stacked. It demonstrates the trust and bond you have with your dog—**teamwork**.

There is another method of free baiting. Instead of keeping your dog on the mat in the usual horizontal position, push the dog out vertically toward the center of the ring. You can even go to the extreme of pushing the dog off the mat. The judge cannot help noticing you and your dog. However, I cannot stress the importance of subtlety. Some judges will not appreciate this form of upstaging. Be discreet.

The art of showing dogs is not based only on ability, but also on mental stability. If you become nervous or apprehensive, your dog may become nervous as well because of your close bond. You must be certain not to let your apprehension extend down the lead to your dog. Relaxing in the ring will relieve your stress and that of your dog, and it will make your time together a more pleasurable experience regardless of the outcome.

The Best Handlers Disappear

General Douglas MacArthur stated: "Old soldiers never die, they just fade away." The same can be said about good handlers. The very best disappear—**behind** their dogs.

The AKC Guidelines state clearly that in Junior Showmanship the dog is to be presented in the same manner as in the breed ring. And, one of the purposes of Junior Showmanship is to prepare the young exhibitor for showing in the classes.

A handler, whether in the breed ring or Junior Showmanship, should strive to become invisible when showing his dog. What we mean by this is that the dog should always be in the forefront. The handler's technique and style should never be exaggerated to draw the judge's attention away from his dog. You are showing the *dog*, not yourself.

Your movements and corrections should always be subtle, and you should avoid fussing excessively over your dog. Your goal is to give the impression of the dog showing himself. It might be prudent to make a more noticeable correction at some time during the class, just to let the judge know that yours is not a push-button performance.

As you practice your skills and become a team with your dog, your performance will begin to flow more smoothly. You will find that there is no great secret to successfully disappearing behind your dog. Smoothness and subtlety are the key ingredients.

Conclusion

Winning consistently in Junior Showmanship requires a smooth, highly polished, confident display of teamwork between dog and handler on a continual basis. These goals can only be accomplished through practice, hard work and perseverance. When in the ring, the good handler must be alert at all times, be prepared to make quick decisions and execute them skillfully.

The handler, Kylie Jo Wolkenheim, demonstrates perfectly the concept of disappearing behind the dog. Please note that the dog is the focal point of the photograph. (Photo by Downey)

Chapter 8
Patience, Perseverance, Persistence

It was the best of times. It was the worst of times. —Charles Dickens

That quote sums up my junior showmanship career pretty well, perhaps even dog shows in general. We have learned throughout this book that Junior Showmanship teaches many virtues: discipline, good sportsmanship, patience, and the list goes on, but there is one thing that can be held in higher esteem and that is persistence. Never give up no matter the circumstances. Even if it doesn't pay off in the winning department at least you know you gave it everything you had. You did not let your dog or yourself down. Two good examples of the notion happen to be Olympic moments.

1988 marked the first year of the Jamaican Bobsled Team. They were the object of ridicule. During their final run, they were speeding down the hill at World Record pace when the track on their sled loosened and caused the sled to flip. Instead of getting angry and just letting their hard work seem for nothing, they picked up their sled and carried it to the finish line.

At the '92 Barcelona Olympics, British runner, Derek Redmond, pulled a hamstring halfway through the 400 meter qualifying heat. He collapsed to the track in pain not so much physically as mentally because his Olympic dreams were dashed, but not completely. His father came down from the stands and helped him to the finish line to complete the race.

These athletes did not win on these particular occasions, but they persevered through adversity and finished what they started.

Many times throughout my juniors' career I came across judges who put me down for showing a little dog. They thought showing a big dog was more difficult than showing a little one. When I got my Springer, I found out she was no more difficult to show than my Lhasas. The only thing that separates dogs is their personality. Their minds, not their size or flashiness. It was the mind of my dogs with which I had to contend on several occasions. These occasions started out as the worst times, but somehow ended up as the best times.

The first bad experience I had was in novice junior. I was in a large class, and the judge wanted catalog order. Naturally I was stuck in between two large dogs. I really had had no experience with this type of situation since I was just a novice junior. The class started moving around and we got half way around the ring when the German Shepherd behind us turned out to be too much for his handler. He cut the corner and ran us over. All I could think was that Toby would not show. I figured his tail would be down and never hang over his back again. I relied upon instinct and put trust in my dog. I pulled Toby off the mat, facing the gate so I shielded him from the oncoming traffic. When the last dog passed me I patted Toby on the back and off we went. He showed like nothing ever happened, and we ended up winning our third first place. That was still in the days when you could transfer right up into open junior. I ended up winning the open junior class as well. I would have had best junior, but the judge introduced me to my first "L," and I did not switch hands out of ignorance.

Toby was one of my best juniors' dogs, although I really did not ever have a bad junior's dog. It's just some were a little more difficult than others—like Chad. Chad was a stubborn Lhasa, and you have not lived until you have tried to show one of these guys. He could hold a grudge for a long time. He would get mad at me and fix me by relieving himself in the ring. That would not have been so bad, but he never learned to lift his leg. He squatted like a female and if I had a dime for every person who told me what a wonderful girl he was, I'd be rich! That was his way of getting even with me. I could always sense a smile lurking around those dark lips of his. The worst experience I had with him was when I was in open junior. I had won that class and was in competing for best junior. Chad was about 10 months old and he still liked to take afternoon naps. I had him stacked up and all of a sudden he decided it was naptime and that he wouldn't work anymore. I was

Taking a sigh of relief and a victory photo on the day Cricket decided to make her worst. (Booth Photo)

left holding Chad up under the chin and by the base of his tail to keep him from lying down as his legs had gone completely limp. I figured for sure best junior was out of the question with this situation occurring, but I ended up winning it. The judge commented afterward that he saw what was going on and liked the fact that I didn't get flustered despite Chad's digressions.

Michael got me to the one place I never expected at the World Series of Junior Showmanship. It is ironic that the event he got me to was the one that ended up burning him out for dog shows. It was a few months after the World Series when Michael had his last show. A couple of weeks before, he had blown a five-point major because he acted up in the show ring. He was not himself, and physically there was nothing wrong with him. I didn't realize until after he pulled a stunt in juniors that he was just plain burned out. From the minute I stepped into the open senior class I knew I was in trouble. Michael didn't want to stack. He kept moving his legs and would hold one up in the air and refuse to put it down. Now, Michael was one of those dogs that just flowed around the ring. Not that day. He moved so slowly a snail could have passed him by. No matter what I tried, he did not want to do it. The whole class was like that for us—a struggle until the end. He would not cooperate, and I kept fighting. My persistence paid off because I won that day.

Cricket, my Springer, was my toughest challenge. She was not a push-button dog. She had her own ideas of how things should be done, and if I made her mad before we showed, like Chad, she would get even. It was at a Memorial Day cluster that my greatest challenge would occur. Cricket acted like a beast on the grooming table while I was getting her ready to go in the ring. She kept moving her feet so I could not trim the few hairs sticking out. In her eyes, that was big mistake. I paid dearly, but lucky for her, persistence prevailed.

The open senior class was large and immediately Cricket refused to stack. She began posting and slouching so that she made me look inept. The judge was walking down the line, and I had this big mess. I got her somewhat stacked, but kept fighting with her for every repair. So when the judge moved the class around, Cricket decided to amble. I gave a light jerk on the lead, and she only slowed down more. By now, Cricket, an English Springer, was being passed up by little dogs. The entire class was a battle for me to make this dog look decent. I don't think we ever achieved "decent" that day. She looked horrible and it was her own doing. I did everything possible to make her look good short of beating her over the head with my pin brush. Throughout the entire class, I just kept thinking of which methods I would employ to kill her once we left the showsite. It was the first time I ever wanted to kill a dog, even though it was figurative.

The judge asked us to take our dogs into the middle of the ring and "sell our dogs." There were kids in there with perfect little soldiers who free baited like a dream. And there I was with a dog I had "to sell," and I was willing to pay someone to take her. So when my turn came around, I went into the center of the ring with her and MADE her self-stack. I swear it took me five minutes and the judge allowed me the time to get her to free bait and finally she cooperated slightly. I knew I was going to go last. I had one of the worst performances of my entire juniors career, and yet the judge pulled me out first. We took the class, and I fought my way to a best junior win too. It was the most unexpected win I ever had. The judge said when he marked his book," That was a hard dog to handle." He wasn't kidding either. I never lost my cool or gave up. I fought until the end and was rewarded for my handling skills. Skills that are the cornerstone of successful handling.

The cornerstone to a successful team is trust and respect. A dog must trust his handler and a handler must trust his dog in order for mutual respect to develop. That is the hardest relationship to achieve, but well worth the effort.

Michael was an enthusiastic dog. He was nearly four years old and had not matured. It's what I like to call the "Peter Pan" syndrome. He was good at galloping rather than trotting. He just wanted to gait at full force. This became a problem so I decided it was time to bring in a choker. For three months I worked with him on a choke collar. Since it was during the lull of the dog show season, I just worked him at home. I decided that it was time to test him without the choke and graduate him to a martingale. The test was the Detroit Kennel Club Show, not only our first show of the year and a World Series qualifier, but the first in which he would be without a choker. I decided to treat this show as a practice session. There was no pressure. I exercised a great deal of trust in Michael by switching him to a martingale. It paid off. He put on the performance of a lifetime, and we were on our way to Beverly Hills.

Boots, I would have to say, was my best junior's dog. He was a born natural and anything I taught only needed to be done once. He picked up new things easily. He was the first dog I taught the "blind courtesy turn." I never trusted a dog as much as I did him. He always gave 120 percent and never failed me. Our routines were smooth only because I never had to ask him to do a turn or free bait. He always knew. He anticipated every move. The turns on the "L" especially became so imbedded in his mind there were a few times that he actually did the turn a second before we were supposed to.

Willie was the dog I put complete trust in at a time when it was considered to be a big gamble. It was my last year of juniors, and I had seven wins. I still had more than two months before I aged out, but I wanted that last win to qualify for Westminster to keep the pressure off. So, on the day of the show I looked over the catalog. I knew my competition, but I also knew I needed to do something to give me an edge. I decided outside the ring during Novice Junior to teach Willie the "blind courtesy turn." We had never practiced it before and I was not sure how he would react to something new. We practiced a few times and he seemed to have it so I left it at that. It was a warm day, and he was heavy coated. I didn't want him overheating before we ever got into the ring. We showed and keeping with the pattern of her other classes, the judge asked us to do a "down and back" on our individual. I stayed cool on the outside, but inside I prayed Willie would do the turn. He did and we won because of it. I'll never forget the judge's reaction when we did that turn. She thought it was the neatest thing she had ever seen.

I never believed the saying, "You can't teach an old dog new tricks," until I met Cricket. When I first got Cricket, she did not respect me. She didn't respect me enough to listen to me. She was the boss. I was no one in her eyes. It was a six-month battle of getting an older dog back into show condition, retraining and earning her respect and my trust. Our first show experience was a complete disaster. At class, and at home, we did quite well. I still was not used to showing a sporting dog, and I knew it would take time. Cricket did not help things either. At our first show, she did everything possible to humiliate me. She would not stack or move, and I could see her laughing the whole time. I was about ready to give her back to her co-owner.

We practiced and trained constantly. I worked on teaching her the "blind courtesy turn" and she did it beautifully at home. A month later, I took her to a show and figured she was ready to do the turn in competition. We went about our routine and on our "down and back" I signaled for her to do the turn, but she refused. She put on the brakes like a horse refusing a jump. It felt like a five-minute battle, but I made her do that turn. It was not pretty and as I expected we went third out of three. I learned that Cricket would never be taught anything new again. It wasn't that she was stupid. To her, it was fine to throw it in during practice, but when we were in the ring things had to be done the old way. It took awhile, but when I finally did earn her respect she made up for the lousy performances.

Trust and respect are the key to successful team work and to a career of longevity. To get the most out of your dog these virtues must be on a mutual basis.

Chapter 9
Sportsmanship

The Junior Showmanship world of the nineties has evolved into a highly competitive and tension-filled sport. In past decades, winning Best Junior Handler at Westminster Kennel Club Show was the most highly coveted award. With the introduction of the World Series of Junior Showmanship and more recently the PEDIGREE® Junior Showmanship National Invitational, there is more at stake for Juniors than ever before. The all-expense-paid trips to the Finals Competition, Crufts, and the World Show, plus the increased monetary values of other prizes awarded and the ramifications of winning a qualifier, have increased the pressures on the junior handler today. It can be very easy to lose perspective of what is really most important. This chapter will give you some insight into what is acceptable and expected behavior in the Junior Showmanship ring and advice on how to become a better sportsman.

Be Friendly and Help Others
Friendships in Junior Showmanship can be established in many different ways. They can result from a simple conversation at ringside, or while waiting in the ring during a large class. Once you become acquainted with your fellow exhibitors, you will find that most of them have feelings and goals very similar to your own. As these friendships develop, you may be able to assist one another in improving your skills.

When you are in the show ring, you are experiencing your performance from a one-dimensional perspective, yours. A friend positioned inside (or outside) the ring perceives a three-dimensional picture and sees you from the same viewpoint as the judge. Because of this advantage, your friend can give you important pointers on how you can improve or polish your skills. You, in turn, can do the same for them when they are in the ring. A simple word from a friend could realistically turn today's loss into tomorrow's victory.

By helping one another, you establish a teamwork effort that can greatly enhance your enjoyment of the sport. If it is not your day to win, you can take pleasure in the wins of your friends. When it is your turn to win, they can take pleasure in yours. Friendship can help bring the most important purpose of Junior Showmanship back into focus; i.e., winning does not have to be the most important objective. This is a much healthier outlook.

When you see a newcomer make an obvious mistake while showing in Junior Showmanship, take him aside later and let him know. Many of these children do not have the advantage of training classes and must learn as they go. By helping them, you are also setting the right example for them to follow.

If you show a friendly face to the world and help others whenever possible, you will be practicing the most important aspect of Junior Showmanship.

Don't Get Caught up in Petty Gossip

When you have been involved in the dog show world long enough, you will find that the dog show grapevine is one of the quickest sources of communication in the world. Gossip is a way of life for many exhibitors; unfortunately, it filters down into the Junior Showmanship ring.

The height of bad sportsmanship is gossiping about other exhibitors, especially if one also happens to be the winner of the day. It is a vicious and hurtful habit, and one that should not be pursued. You would not enjoy hearing unpleasant rumors about yourself; so why contribute to the hurt of another.

Consequently, avoid getting caught up in the world of petty jealousy and gossip. Remember that everyone has feelings and respect them!

Be a Good Loser

Regardless of your abilities as a junior handler, you will do your fair share of winning and losing. How you conduct yourself in each situation will tell others a great deal about you, not only as a handler, but as a person. It is much easier to be a graceful winner than a graceful loser. However, the face you show to the world when you lose, which will be approximately 90 percent of the time, is the one people will see and remember the most.

Losing is always difficult to accept, especially in Junior Showmanship, because judging is based on your merit as a handler. It is you, not the dog, that is being judged. So naturally, a loss can feel like a personal attack. It can be frustrating at times because you know you have shown to the best of your ability.

There are times when you know you should have won. The hint of politics may come to your mind, possibly with good reason. Or you may feel the judge just did not know what he was doing. All of these things may be true at one time or another, but dwelling on them will not change anything. Allowing yourself to get angry or lose control is a waste of time and energy.

Being a good handler requires a great deal of self-discipline. If you are old enough to show a dog, you are old enough to control your temper. In the beginning, it will be more difficult to control your feelings; however, if you keep your temper in check, you will find each loss easier to accept than the one before. When you graduate to the breed ring and start showing against the adults, temper tantrums will not be tolerated. So you may as well learn to control your feelings. It will be a valuable lesson learned, and one that many adults have yet to master.

Learning to lose with grace builds character and develops self-discipline. If you feel disappointed after a loss, try to put things back into perspective. This was only **one** show, and **one** judge, giving **one** opinion. Life is filled with tomorrows, and your day in the spotlight will come. In the meantime, relax, enjoy the time with your dog, keep your temper in control, and continue to practice and improve your skills. You might just discover you are a winner in more ways than one!

Be an Even Better Winner

There are few experiences as uplifting as a good win in Junior Showmanship. You are at the top of the world! God loves you! You are invincible! At least for the day.

There is nothing wrong with displaying your pleasure when you win, but be discreet and handle your success with humility. Do not gloat, scream, yell or furiously jump for joy. While you are busy celebrating, take a long, hard look at the faces surrounding you! You may be the victor, but they are the defeated. The faces you are looking at are a mirror image of your own on the days that you were not the winner. Do not forget.

No matter how strong a friendship is between two juniors, it will be natural to display some disappointment at losing, even if it is to your friend. Keep these thoughts in mind as you are waiting in line for the judge to give you your ribbons and prizes, as show photos are being taken, or as you return to the grooming area. Be considerate of the other juniors' feelings. Don't gloat and don't patronize. There is nothing as insulting to a person's intelligence as syrupy, meaningless compliments, things that would never be said if the tables were turned.

In Junior Showmanship, and the dog world in general, you will find that there are many types of friendship. You will tend to be everyone's friend when you are losing, and friend to a very few when you win. Friendships that can survive the give and take of winning and losing are true friendships. People of this caliber are to be complimented and have earned the right to be called friend.

Those people who are fair-weather friends are not a loss. You never really had them as friends in the first place. Be cordial to them in the future, and definitely congratulate them when they win, even if they don't return the favor. Following their example only lowers you to their negative level of sportsmanship. Your goal should be to aspire to the heights of sportsmanship, not the lows.

On the days when you are the winner, accept your prizes, compliments, and congratulations gracefully. Let it all end as you leave the ring. If you feel the need to celebrate, do so later when the others are not around. Treat others as you would like to be treated. It makes it a great deal easier for the other exhibitors to accept their losses when the winner is not an obnoxious boor.

Be Courteous to the Judge and Other Exhibitors

Whenever individuals vie for a prize, which only one can win, there will be competition. Winning is an important aspect of any competitive sport; however, as the old adage states, "it is how you play the game" that is most important. As corny as it may sound, this philosophy embraces a great deal of truth.

One of the most difficult aspects of Junior Showmanship is learning to hide your emotions, especially when you lose. There will be many occasions when you will disagree with the judging. However, when entering a dog show, you are paying for a judge's opinion. Whether you agree with his opinions or not, you must learn to control your emotions and accept his decisions.

Once the placements have been assigned, a good sport **always** congratulates the winner. Regardless of who the winner is (friend or foe), he or she deserves this common courtesy. The ability to congratulate the winner gracefully will strengthen your character and establish a good reputation with your fellow exhibitors. Venting your anger and taking your frustrations out on the winner is the coward's way out. Tomorrow may be your day in the spotlight, and you won't appreciate your moment being tarnished by someone else's ill feelings. Respect breeds respect. Set the example, and you will find that those around you will follow your lead.

When you are not the winner, it is difficult to stand in line waiting for the judge to hand out the ribbons. So much emphasis is placed on being first that it is natural (at times) to feel disappointment at a lower placement. The fact that it was a large class, or that you have beaten many good junior handlers may be little comfort. Nevertheless, there is no other acceptable reaction than to accept your loss with grace and dignity.

Proper etiquette requires that we treat our elders with respect. Judges warrant respect because of their position. Many judges are retired professional handlers, breeders, owner-handlers or past juniors with years of experience to back up their decisions.

Judges are human beings and despite what you may think, they have feelings too. Most judges take Junior Showmanship very seriously and perform their tasks to the best of their abilities. As individuals, they have the right to their own opinions and preferences. Just because you do not agree does not mean they are wrong.

On days when you feel uncertain as to why you have lost, approach the judge and ask for a critique. You may find he has sound reasons for giving you the placement you received. He can supply you with constructive criticisms you can apply to your present handling skills that will later assist you in attaining high placements. Some of the greatest lessons you learn in life arise from the ashes of our mistakes.

When the judge hands you a placement ribbon, smile pleasantly, say thank you and leave the ring in a composed manner. Many junior (and adult) exhibitors make the mistake of grabbing the ribbon, saying thank you in a curt manner, and stomping out of the ring. The ribbon is then promptly deposited in the nearest trash container. Not only does this display of bad temper leave a bad impression, but it shows a total lack of respect for the judge and fellow exhibitors, and also for oneself. It may be in your future to show to this judge again. Why burn your bridges with bad behavior?

Self-discipline relates to many areas of Junior Showmanship and the handling world. You must not only practice your patterns and other handling skills, but also the control necessary to keep your temper in check. How you handle your dog is as important as how you handle your emotions. Accomplishing both will make you a winner not only in the show ring, but as a person.

Never Crowd Out Other Exhibitors

When stacking your dog in the ring, leave enough room between yourself and fellow exhibitors. Not only does this show consideration, but it gives you the room to move freely around your dog when necessary. Over the years, I have observed juniors climbing over their dogs' backs, or bumping into other exhibitors because they failed to judge how much room they would need.

Occasionally, a junior's judge will walk between the dogs while they are stacked in line. By not allowing enough room for him to get around, you not only lessen your chance of winning, but you will also hurt your neighbor's chances.

You may find the occasional junior who will deliberately attempt to crowd you as a form of upstaging, thinking "if the judge cannot see you, he cannot put you up." This is a very unsportsmanlike attitude, and just might be very effective in eliminating you from the competition. "Crowding out" does not occur in Junior Showmanship very often; however, if you find yourself the victim of this tactic, calmly ask the offender to allow you more room. If he refuses or cannot do it, keep cool, and make the best of the situation. When judging has been completed and you have left the ring, take the handler aside and tell him in a composed, but firm, manner that you did not appreciate the crowding and to refrain from doing so in the future.

Never Intentionally Run up on Someone Else's Dog

Sportsmanship comes in many forms. It is not just applied to the art of being a graceful winner and loser, but to the way you treat fellow competitors. One of the few unforgivable sins in handling is intentionally running up on a competitor's dog. Some exhibitors have a total lack of confidence in their dogs or handling capabilities, and they feel the need to use this dirty trick to give them the edge. This is cruel and unsportsmanlike behavior, as it can injure a competitor's dog or frighten the dog so badly that he may not want to show again that day, or ever. In addition, the handler could also be hurt if he trips or falls. Fortunately, most incidents of "running up" on a competitor's dog in Junior Showmanship are purely accidental, often a mistake made by a novice because he has so many things to remember and is easily distracted.

To avoid such incidents, take a good look at what types of dogs you have in front and behind you as you line up in the ring at the beginning of the class. These observations can give you a basic idea of the pace required by each dog so you can make the appropriate adjustments when you gait your dog with the group.

Many judges in Junior Showmanship arrange the dogs according to size, and in these instances you can gauge the pace quite accurately. However, other judges prefer catalog order, especially in larger classes—in order to keep the class more organized. In this type of situation, your handling skills and instincts will be greatly tested. If you have a large dog and are surrounded by little dogs, or the reverse, you may have problems. Whatever the case, allow yourself a 10-second reaction time, or let the dog in front of you get a mat's length start before you begin gaiting your dog. This accomplishes two things. First, it allows you to show your dog at his best pace. Second, if the handler in front of you suddenly stops (or is having problems) you have enough time to react, and avoid inadvertently running up on him.

If you are in the ring with an exhibitor that runs up on your dog, do not get angry or flustered. Turn to the exhibitor and nicely tell him what he has done, and to please be careful in the future. If he still persists, tell him again more firmly. If it becomes obvious that words will not rectify the situation, you have only one acceptable alternative—get out of the situation gracefully. One of my instructors gave me the following simple solution when this situation occurs. If you have a brush or comb in the ring, drop it as the group prepares to gait. As you go to pick it up, accidentally kick it off the mat towards the middle of the ring. This diversion will allow you enough time for the group to pass you by, then you can smoothly move to the rear of the line and gait your dog without the poor sport behind you. If you do not have a brush or comb, your armband can be substituted.

Avoid Making Excessive Noise in the Ring

There are many unwritten rules in the worlds of etiquette and common courtesy. When showing your dog, it is a matter of common courtesy to refrain from making excessive noise in the ring. Bangle bracelets and other types of jewelry that make noise should not be worn while showing. In addition, carrying noisy change or keys in your pockets should also be avoided. The excessive or unexpected noises these items make can be annoying for other exhibitors and distracting or frightening to their dogs or your own. Large amounts of change can spill from shallow pockets during gaiting and create havoc in the ring and embarrassment for the handler. The noise from shoes that clack or clump in the ring can also be disturbing to the dog directly in front of you in the ring.

Before coming to the ring, empty your pockets of any potential noisemakers and wear sensible shoes. If you should forget, the dog you frighten may be your own.

Keep Your Bait to Yourself

Bait can be a useful tool for getting your dog's attention, but it can also be a nuisance, especially when it ends up on the floor in the ring. The bait can draw the attention of the other exhibitors' dogs, resulting in the dogs sniffing the ground and upsetting their handlers. Exhibitors might step on leftover bait in the ring, embedding it into the grooves of the mats and making it difficult for the show-giving club to clean. Littering the ring with bait also angers many judges.

Meggin Guthrie provides an example of baiting without littering.

Be considerate when in the show ring, and keep your bait to yourself. If you must throw it to gain your dog's attention, be a good sport, and pick it up.

Several years ago, I learned through firsthand experience the disadvantage of exhibiting in the same ring with an inconsiderate handler. It was the first weekend I showed my Springer, Cricket, and I had her stacked in line as the judge was looking over the class. It was a large class, and it took him a while to reach the end of the line. The junior behind me was baiting her dog and threw the bait, causing it to land underneath my dog. Cricket is a "chow hound" and has yet to meet a food she does not like. I knew if she discovered the bait beneath her, it would create a major problem. Needless to say, this junior's lack of courtesy frustrated me, so I picked up the bait and threw it right back at her. They say a "picture is worth a thousand words," and I have to say the look on her face spoke volumes. She was appalled at my reaction; however, my reaction demonstrated how distracting bait pitching can be, and she did not repeat the action again in my presence.

When using bait, use it wisely. Do not pitch bait around like Nolan Ryan. Just keep it in your pocket until you are ready to use it. If you see a piece on the floor, even if it is not yours, pick it up and throw it away.

Keep Your Dog Comfortable in the Warm Weather

It was a typical spring day in Kentucky—hot and humid. The sun was at its highest point as the Junior Showmanship classes began. There were few juniors properly prepared for the unseasonably warm climate, or for the needs of their dogs.

I was waiting outside the ring with Cricket, my Springer, and her basic necessities for the day: a stainless steel bucket (filled with water), a wet towel, and a spray bottle filled with water. As the classes progressed, many dogs became uncomfortable, and some of them were beginning to overheat. A dog is not able to talk, but signs such as excessive and rapid panting, noisy breathing, bright red tongue, drooling of thick saliva, and weakness with a wobbly gait are warnings that your dog is in trouble, and action should be taken immediately. One handler, who was in the Novice Senior class, obviously did not recognize these symptoms and was having trouble keeping her dog under control in the ring. She was not catering to his needs, and because of his discomfort, he was becoming aggressive toward her and the judge. Consequently, the judge excused her and the dog because of her ignorance and lack of compassion.

A successful outing on a hot, muggy, Kentucky afternoon. (Baines Photo)

After a long wait, the Open Senior class was finally called into the ring, and I was a little concerned. Cricket does not do well in excessive heat; and even though I had her under the tent as much as possible, she was still showing signs of discomfort. As we waited in line, I placed the wet towel over her back to cool her down, and squirted some of the water from the spray bottle into her mouth to replace lost fluids and make her more comfortable. As a result of the warm weather, I felt our performance was adequate, but not inspiring. When we were through gaiting, I returned her to the comfort of the shade and put her towel back in place. To my surprise, I won Best Junior Handler that day.

As we were taking the show photographs, the judge explained to me why he had excused the girl in the Novice Senior class. He told me it was very apparent to him that my dog's needs were being taken care of in the ring because her topcoat was damp to the touch when he examined her. This happened to be one of the reasons why I won. He also stated that *the dog's comfort should always come first*, and that it was a very sad fact that many handlers forget these simple needs.

There are many ways you can make your dog more comfortable in hot weather. Your dog should be well-exercised so that he does not embarrass you by eliminating in the ring. However, your dog should not be gaited excessively or allowed to romp and play excessively. This type of activity will overheat him before you ever get into the ring.

If the weather is extremely hot, after you groom your dog, keep him in an air-conditioned motor home, trailer, van or car as close to ring time as possible. If you have a small dog, carry him to ringside instead of making him walk; or if your dog is larger, walk him more slowly to the ring to conserve his energy.

At ringside you will need the following equipment: a towel, icepack, and a spray bottle filled with plain water. If you have a shorthaired breed, you can drape a wet towel over his back until it is time for you to go into the ring. Longer haired dogs can be kept cool by letting them lie on ice packs wrapped in a towel. Offer your dog plenty of water to drink. A bottle of Gatorade at ringside for yourself wouldn't be a bad idea either.

While you are in the ring, try to keep your dog under the tent in the shade whenever possible. If the judge does not allow you to go under the tent, or if there is not shade, kneel in front of your dog to block out as much sun as possible. Hang your bottle and wet towel on the fencing around the ring so that you can easily reach them to give your dog a drink or a quick cool down while waiting during the class.

Most importantly, do not push your dog to perform beyond his capabilities in warm weather. If the judge decides to overlook your performance because your dog did not move as quickly as another, or with more animation, so be it. It is better to have no placing at all, than to have a dog that wins and then collapses from heat exhaustion.

Being a good sport is not just congratulating the winners, or being respectful of the judges and your fellow exhibitors. It is also recognizing and fulfilling the needs of your dog. Remember, your dog is your partner. Treat him with kindness and consideration, and he will reward you 10 times over with his love and cooperation.

Winning is Never More Important than Your Dog's Comfort

Competitiveness is a common characteristic of any sport. It can be that something extra that gives a person the drive and confidence to perform at maximum capability. There are many athletes, professional and amateur, that take competitiveness to its highest level and will compete even when injured. However, in the world of dog shows the dogs are the athletes, and they should never compete when they are injured or ill.

The AKC and veterinarians frown on owners who show ill or injured dogs, especially if the illness is communicable. If your dog is actively ill and you bring him to a show anyway, you could infect any number of dogs through your own thoughtlessness. In addition, a sick dog's immune system is lowered making him more susceptible to secondary infection. If a dog is injured and limping in the ring, the judge is required by AKC to excuse the dog from the class.

In 1989, the AKC changed the rules and regulations for Junior Showmanship to allow for such occurrences. If a dog is ill or injured, a junior may substitute another dog that meets ownership and eligibility requirements, provided application is made to the superintendent at least one half hour before the start of all judging for that day. This also applies to bitches that come in season, as they are ineligible to be shown during this time.

If you have only one dog to show, it is best not to jeopardize his health for the sake of a possible win. There will always be other dog shows.

Never Take Your Anger or Frustrations Out on Your Dog

Regardless of how well you and your dog perform as a team, there will be days when your performance will not be inspired. Your dog may decide he knows a better way to do a pattern, or may get even with you because of some indignity you performed on the grooming table before judging. Sometimes there is no reason, except for one that is lost forever between two fuzzy ears. Whatever the reason, you must not get frustrated over these lapses in good judgment on the part of your dog. It happens to the best handlers, professional or amateur, and you may as well learn to take these events in your stride, because it will inevitably happen again.

Getting angry with your dog because of misbehavior in the ring is a wasted emotion. Dogs forget their misdeeds very quickly, and if you are going to make a correction they will understand, it must be performed immediately after the inappropriate action. It is not necessary to make rough or heavy-handed corrections, especially if it is to satisfy your own anger at the dog. Over-reacting to minor infractions is the quickest way to sour your dog on dog showing. Your heavy-handed corrections will teach him that showing hurts and that it is not a pleasant way to spend the day.

On days that you do not win, regardless of whether it is your dog's fault or not, you should never take your disappointment out on him. Junior Showmanship is judged on how you handle your dog, not on how your dog behaves. If he misbehaves, the judge will watch to see your reaction and judge you accordingly. Displaying anger or frustration will not get you high marks; it will only show your inexperience.

Good sportsmanship also encompasses how you treat your dog. The next time you get angry at him or frustrated, just remember, if it weren't for your dog, you would not be able to compete in Junior Showmanship at all. He is your partner; so treat him with the respect he deserves. You will discover that he will love you for it!

Sportsmanship and the American Kennel Club

In 1992, the AKC began enforcing its rules and regulations regarding sportsmanship at dog shows and all AKC events.

The AKC desires that all exhibitors behave with proper decorum to set a good example for the general public visiting a dog show for the first time. Temper tantrums, loud and unruly altercations between individuals, profanity of any kind, violence toward another person or animal are some of the areas of concern. Moreover, the judges must always be treated with respect, and your opinions of them and their judging must be kept to yourself until you leave the show grounds. If you are charged with any of these infractions, you face the prospect of being tried by a bench committee. If you are found guilty, you can sustain not only a fine, but also a suspension from all AKC privileges for an indeterminate time.

Being a good sport has many advantages. Showing your dogs, enjoying the friendship and camaraderie of fellow exhibitors, the joy of winning, and spending time with your dog are just a few examples. Is a momentary lapse of good behavior really worth jeopardizing any of these privileges?

Conclusion

Being a good sport is more than just congratulating the winner. It is the ability to be a good winner as well as a good loser. It encompasses friendship, courtesy toward judges and fellow exhibitors and their dogs. And, most importantly, it means taking care of the needs of your dog.

Junior Showmanship skills can carry over into the breed ring. Kari Wuornos pictured winning a Group I under Mrs. Sari Brewster Tiejen. (Photo by Graham)

Chapter 10
A Guide for Junior Showmanship Parents

As a retired Junior Showmanship mother, I can give you a firsthand account of what you will encounter as a Junior Showmanship parent and what your responsibilities will be. In the past 10 years, the Junior Showmanship ring has evolved into a highly competitive, sometimes ruthless, extraordinarily polished arena. The World Series of Junior Showmanship and more recently the Pedigree-sponsored National Invitational Junior Showmanship Competition have added a new dimension to the world of Junior Showmanship in the United States. The prizes and ramifications of winning can place enormous pressures on the young junior. As adults, we find the pressures of showing our dogs in the breed classes unsettling at times. Junior handlers, without benefit of an adult's years of experience and maturity, can find the pressures overwhelming. It will be up to you, as the adult in the relationship, to help your junior handler keep winning and losing in perspective and deal with the ups and downs of competing. This is true even if you are a novice in the dog game.

During the eight years my daughter, Anne, competed in Junior Showmanship, we attended more dog shows than I can remember. The one aspect of attending all those shows that I will not forget is the quality time that we spent together doing something we both enjoyed. Some days, weekends, months and years were more enjoyable than others, but we found that each new adventure was also a new learning experience—an experience shared.

The long car rides home from the shows allowed us the time to discuss the events of the day and to put them into perspective. On the

Another junior handler, Melissa Hall, is shown winning a Group I.(Booth Photo)

days Anne was successful, the rides home always seemed shorter and more enjoyable. On the less successful days, the drive home could be interminable. However, we would try to leave the pain of losing behind and talk about other things which seemed to shorten the trip. It would seem hard to believe, but there was a world outside of Junior Showmanship!

In many cases, the losing days were a greater learning experience than the winning days. Brooding over a loss was wasted emotion and did not change anything. So we tried to use the loss to Anne's advantage, which was a more positive outlet for her frustrations. Once she was ready, we would discuss the show and compare notes regarding the judging. In most cases, we were able to figure out exactly what the judge was doing and what he was looking for. When we realized this, we were able to analyze her performance and make corrections where necessary. During the weeks between shows, she would practice those areas of her handling skills that we felt needed to be sharpened. This routine led to a steady improvement in her skills as a handler, her attitude toward losing, and her sportsmanship throughout her Junior Showmanship career. I cannot say that we agreed with every judgment and learned from every experience; however, our goal was to always try to remain objective.

Children learn through example. The face you present to the world when you lose will be the face you see each time your child wins or loses in Junior Showmanship. If you are a graceful winner and a dignified loser, you are setting the proper example for your junior handler to emulate. However, if you become sullen and angry when you lose, criticize the judge and your competitors, you can rest assured that you will witness that exact behavior outside the Junior Showmanship ring on a losing day. As adults, we must constantly be on our guard to be proper role models.

When Anne was competing in Junior Showmanship, I would note some parents who were overzealous in their support of their junior handlers. When the junior would leave the ring after a particularly dismal performance, they would immediately pounce on them with lists of their many imperfections in the ring that day. The child was in no mood for criticism; so neither parent nor child benefited from this tirade, except possibly as a frustration-release for the parent. On the other side of the coin, there were parents who became so irate with the judging they would storm into the ring afterward and confront the judge.

Not only does this form of behavior put a strain on the parent-child relationship, but it embarrasses the junior in front of his peers and the judge. In addition, these confrontations do not set a good example for junior handlers nor help them place the emphasis of winning and losing in proper perspective. After all, this is only a sporting event that encompasses five minutes of competition—it is not the end of the world!

We all want to see our children succeed in whatever they attempt. It will be only natural for you to want to see your junior win in the Junior Showmanship ring. However, you must be careful not to place too much emphasis on winning. Regardless of how accomplished your junior handler is, he will do his fair share of winning and losing.

When the frustrations of losing begin to build up, give your junior handler something positive to hold onto. Tell him that everything is okay and that tomorrow is another day, even though he will probably groan and roll his eyes at you. Try not to dwell on the negative aspects of his performance. Save the comments for a time and place in which he will be more receptive to criticism. Instead, give him encouragement by complimenting the positive things or improvements over the past few weeks. There may come a time when it will be necessary to pull back and regroup and try and put things into a healthier perspective. It may be wise to encourage your children in other hobbies so that their entire focus does not revolve around dog shows and Junior Showmanship.

Politics in America is a way of life. Anyone who has shown for any length of time will know that politics exists at dog shows. However, winning because of political pull is not as widespread as many would believe. In many instances, an objective overview of the judging can result in a logical explanation for the judge's choices on that day. If you can see a consistency in the winners, where is the politics?

It is a sad fact that politics have filtered down even to the levels of Junior Showmanship. There will be times when you know your child should have won and did not. You will see the wheels of politics in motion and you will stand at ringside as a witness to the injustice. However, there is nothing you can do to change the situation other than not entering your junior under that particular judge again. Do not allow your child to dwell upon losses of this type. Instead, encourage him to practice and refine his skills. This will prepare him for the next time he is confronted with a judge of this sort by making his judging job more difficult. A particularly glowing performance can embarrass a judge into doing the right thing. More importantly, you are giving your child a positive outlook on the situation and teaching him to deal gracefully with the injustices. A lesson he will be able to use as he begins to compete in the breed classes as well as in everyday life.

As my daughter, Anne, reached the end of her career, I did not realize fully what Junior Showmanship had given her until I saw her exhibiting in the Group and Best in Show ring for the first time. At the age of 17, she was awarded a Group One with her English Springer Spaniel the very first time they took the breed. I stood in awe at ringside and watched her in the Group and Best in Show rings doing everything necessary to win. She was totally relaxed and quite at home at this level of competition. At that moment, I realized that Junior Showmanship over the past eight years was merely a dry run for what she was doing now. All of those years of competing with the little kids had prepared her to compete with the big kids. At the age of 17, she had more ring presence, skill and confidence than many adults twice her age or older, including myself. Where else could she have gotten the experience and under-the-gun ring time necessary to learn to compete at this level?

In our lives, Junior Showmanship has always been a love/hate relationship. The introduction to the *Wide World of Sports* on Saturday afternoons sums up the experience nicely: "The thrill of victory and the agony of defeat." At times, you will encounter this circle of emotions

Anne Olejniczak shown finishing a homebred champion with a 5-point specialty major. (Baines Photo)

all in one weekend. Your role will be chauffeur, financial backer, coach, kennel help, grooming assistant, sports psychologist, crying towel and biggest fan. You will be happy, sad, angry, frustrated, bored, and extremely proud—sometimes all in one day. However, I have found that the negative aspects of Junior Showmanship are grossly outweighed by the benefits. Add the fact that both of you will be spending time together building on your relationship, and you might discover Junior Showmanship is a pastime worth pursuing.

Chapter 11
The History of Junior Showmanship

Leonard Brumby Sr. was a man of vision. He was an avid dog fancier, professional handler, and an officer for the Westbury Kennel Club. Mr. Brumby believed that children were the future of the dog world. As such, they should be encouraged to participate actively in dog shows. His idea was to create a competition in which children could compete with one another and be evaluated on their handling abilities. In the late 1920s, he began a campaign to generate support among his associates to establish this form of competition. In 1932, Mr. Brumby's dream was realized with the institution of the first Children's Handling Class at the Westbury Kennel Club Show in Long Island, New York.

The first competition offered separate classes for boys and girls under 14 years of age. In 1933, the age groups were changed to include children under 15 years of age and another class for children under 10 years of age.

Soon the popularity of Children's Handling classes began to grow. Mr. George F. Foley, a dog show superintendent, became an active figure in Children's Handling competitions. Through his encouragement, many of the shows in the Eastern United States began to offer regularly these classes at their events. According to *The American Kennel Club: A Source Book*: "George Foley could be seen quickly trying to explain the Children's Handling Class to a mystified judge." As a result of his involvement in the world of Children's Handling, The George F. Foley Educational Trust was established and provided scholarships for students who were active in the world of dogs and needed financial assistance for college. In 1975, sponsorship of the Foley Trust was assumed by the Dog Writer's Association of America and renamed the Dog Writer's Education Trust (DWET).

In 1933, the Westminster Kennel Club sponsored the first Children's Handling Championship competition. The competition was open to those boys and girls who had earned one first place in Children's Handling during the previous year. Once a junior handler had accumulated three first place wins, he was no longer eligible to compete in the regular Children's Handling classes until after the Westminster Championship. Each year, the winner of the Children's Handling competition was awarded the Grand Challenge Trophy. The Professional Handler's Association sponsored the first Children's Handling Trophy in 1949, which was called *The Leonard Brumby Sr. Memorial Trophy*, in honor of the founder of this event. In 1995, the silver-plated Leonard Brumby Sr. Memorial Trophy was still offered for Best Junior Handler at the Westminster Kennel Club Show. However, the trophy is now sponsored by the Westminster Kennel Club.

The Children's Handling competition began to grow in popularity. Soon these events were held at dog shows throughout the United States and Canada. The Children's Handling competition was officially named Junior Showmanship in 1951.

Judges in the early years of Junior Showmanship were not required to have any special qualifications. Many of the judges were celebrities or movie stars. At his shows, George Foley was again involved with the competition, specifically in the selection of judges. He would go into the crowd and ask a number of professional handlers if they would be willing to judge.

In 1949, Edward Marvin Harrington wrote an article in the September *Gazette* on judging of the Children's Handling Classes. Mr. Harrington felt that even though professional handlers were judging these competitions, there were inconsistencies in judging techniques. Many of his suggestions in that article forged the foundation for judging criteria that are still used in Junior Showmanship today. He recommended the child, not the dog, be judged on the child's handling skills. Judges and other adult members were encouraged to support the efforts of the children, offering advice and trying hard to make the competition a valuable learning experience.

Through the encouragement of the Professional Handlers Association, only licensed professional handlers were allowed to judge. When Junior Showmanship was recognized officially by The American Kennel Club in 1971, judging eligibility was extended to all AKC-licensed judges in addition to licensed handlers. When AKC discontinued licensing for professional handlers in 1974, handlers were no longer eligible to judge Junior Showmanship. In 1995, AKC allowed licensed breed judges and Junior Showmanship judges to preside over Junior Showmanship at any AKC-licensed show. Since 1974, AKC has encouraged former junior handlers to apply for licenses to judge Junior Showmanship.

In 1989, the American Kennel Club instituted a change of rules for Junior Showmanship. At this time, AKC required that all junior handlers obtain a Junior Showmanship I.D. number that must be included on all entry forms. This change also restricted junior handlers from showing bitches in heat in Junior Showmanship. Judges were no longer allowed to base their placement decisions on questions asked of the junior handler on anatomy or general dog information. With bitches in heat being ineligible to show in Junior Showmanship, the AKC allowed the junior handler to substitute another eligible dog prior to judging. If a veterinary certificate is offered, substitutions could be made for dogs that are ill or injured.

Monette Thiele shown placing in Junior Showmanship with her Lhasa Apso at Westminster in her final competition before retirement. (Ashbey Photo)

Chapter 12
Westminster

Every February, on the second Monday and Tuesday, the Westminster Kennel Club hosts its annual show. Next to the Kentucky Derby, the Westminster Kennel Club Dog Show is the second longest running sporting event. In the dog world, Westminster ranks at the same level of prestige as the Derby does in the world of horse racing. Every exhibitor, junior or adult, should experience Westminster and New York City at least once. Despite the crowds and confusion, Westminster has a special charm all its own. It will be an experience long remembered.

For junior handlers, Westminster is one of the greatest tests you will have in mental stamina. My first visit to Westminster was an overwhelming experience, and I know it will be the same for you. Therefore, I will give you a firsthand account of what it is really like to show at Westminster. In this way, your first visit to the Garden will not be as intimidating as my first visit was for me.

Westminster is different from the average dog show in many ways. First, the show is a two-day event that is always held on a Monday and Tuesday. The entry is limited to 2500 dogs because of the limited space available at the showsite. In recent years, the competition has been restricted to finished champions who compete for Best of Breed, Group wins, and Best in Show, and the Junior Showmanship limited entry.

In order for junior handlers to qualify to compete at Westminster, they must have acquired eight first place wins in Open Junior or Open Senior competition during the previous year. The entries are usually accepted by the superintendent by mid-November and close almost immediately, so that a junior handler has to have the eight wins before that time to qualify.

When placing the entry for the show, the junior handler must submit a list of the eight wins with the dates and show names listed. Entries are usually limited to no more than 100 in the Junior Showmanship classes.

The Westminster Kennel Club Show is held in New York City at Madison Square Garden, which is the home of the New York Knicks basketball team and the 1994 Stanley Cup-winning New York Rangers. If you have cable television, some of you may have had the opportunity to watch this show on the USA channel. On the television screen, the showsite appears grand and enormous. However, the reality is that the show could be described as "mass chaos in a crackerbox!"

The rings at Westminster are very small because of the space limitations. Grooming space is limited for the same reason. The show is advertised in the New York newspapers weeks in advance. In 1995, there was even an ad in *People Magazine* advertising the Westminster Kennel Club Show and articles in *USA Today*. As a result, the aisles are crammed with wall-to-wall spectators. "Ready rings" are provided for exhibitors, but the real challenge is getting to them and into the ring on time.

The lights at the Garden are very bright and warm. Add this warmth to the heat generated by the numerous exhibitors and spectators, and the arena can become quite hot. If you live where the climate is cold in the winter, this unseasonable warmth may prove to be a handicap for both you and your dog. Be sure that the clothing you choose is not too warm for these conditions. Wool suits and heavy sweaters can be very uncomfortable. You should also make sure that you have fresh water available at ringside for your dog to drink to keep him from becoming overheated.

The Junior Showmanship classes are usually divided according to which breeds are being judged that day. In the past, working, terrier, non-sporting and herding were judged on Monday while the remaining groups, sporting, hound and toy took place on Tuesday. If you find you will not be able to show on the day you have been assigned, you will be allowed to make alternative arrangements with the superintendent if you contact him before the show.

The Westminster Kennel Club Show, a benched event, requires the dogs to be present at the showsite and on their benches from 11:30 am until 8:00 P.M. Junior Showmanship dogs do not have to be benched in the same manner as the breed-class dogs, and their exhibitors are given special passes to come into the showsite and leave at any time.

However, you must have the dog's entry form provided by the superintendent to get him in and out of the building. Security at the show is very tight to prevent possible dog thefts. Your dog's entry form is your proof to the security staff that you are the dog's owner. Do not lose it!

Before judging takes place, juniors are required to attend a meeting in which ring procedures are explained and may ask questions or make dog substitutions. At this time, the top 20 junior handler ratings are listed for the previous year and Owner-Handler Association Awards are also presented.

Three judges preside over Junior Showmanship at Westminster: two preliminary judges and the finals judge. The preliminary judges will each choose four finalists from their respective groups. The finals judge will then choose Best Junior Handler from this field of eight junior handlers. The final judging takes place on Tuesday evening at 7:30 P.M. in the Group ring prior to the start of Group judging.

Usually the junior handlers are placed in two groups—larger dogs and smaller dogs. One judge will preside over each size. You will never know which judge you will have until you get into the show ring and are divided into groups.

The judging is pretty much the same as in the regular Junior Showmanship classes; however, it takes a great deal longer because of the large number of exhibitors. Showing your dog under these conditions can be very confusing, especially for the first time exhibitor; so be sure to pay close attention to the judge and follow all of his directions. The years that I exhibited at Westminster, the judge divided my class in half. Each half would rest outside the ring while the other was judged.

When you are showing your dog at Westminster, you should remember to stay as relaxed as possible. While you are standing in line awaiting your turn, keep your dog in good position by free-baiting rather than forcing him to stack for long periods of time. The heat and the boredom will inevitably take their toll on your dog's performance and attention span. The goal is to keep him as fresh and alert as possible until it is your turn to be judged. Free-baiting will make your chances of success much greater.

When you are not being judged, be considerate and conserve your dog's strength. Make him sit down and rest, and offer him a drink of fresh water. Pet your dog and play with him a little as you wait. This type of interaction encourages your dog to relax and places his focus on you—a bonus you will appreciate later as you are being judged.

*Anne Olejniczak pictured winning **Best Junior Handler** under Judge **Dr. Charles Garvin.** Dr. Garvin was Best Junior Handler at Westminster in 1969. (Booth Photo)*

Do not be discouraged if your first experiences of Westminster are not everything you had dreamed. Remember that you worked very hard in the previous year for the right to be there. Much of the honor is in getting to Westminster and competing with the nation's best. Think positive, soak up the experience, enjoy yourself. If you get the opportunity to go back again, learn from this experience and make your next visit even more enjoyable and successful!

Westminster Kennel Club Best Junior Handlers

1933	Joseph Sayres: Irish Terrier
1934	Not available.
1935	Joseph Sayres: Irish Terrier
1936	Dorothea McAnulty
1937	Not recorded.
1938	Arthur Mulvihill
1939	Mona Saphir: Old English Sheepdog
1940	Jerry Werber
1941	Betsy Long: Collie
1942	Betty Hinks
1943	Walter Wilson: Gordon Setter
1944	Betty Bolger
1945	Evelyn Staubmueller
1946	Frank Hill
1947	John Herr
1948	George Metz: Boston Terrier
1949	Monica Rumpf
1950	Hope Johnson
1951	Theodore Hallender
1952	William Henry
1953	Phyllis Campbell: Great Dane
1954	George Alston: Boxer
1955	Mary Donnelly: Irish Terrier
1956	Patricia Leary: Afghan
1957	Patricia Matson: Springer Spaniel
1958	Nancy Kelly: Golden Retriever
1959	Bethny Hall: Irish Setter
1960	Allen Kirk: Scottish Terrier
1961	Betty Lou Ham: Irish Setter

1962	Susan Heckmann: Dachshund
1963	Lydia Ceccarine: Boxer
1964	Clare Hodge: Whippet
1965	Jennifer Sheldon: Afghan
1966	Laura Swyler: Wire-haired Dachshund
1967	David Lynn Brumbaugh: Miniature Schnauzer
1968	Cheryl Baker: Pointer
1969	Charles Garvin: Dalmation
1970	Patricia Hardy: Golden Retriever
1971	Heidi Shellenbarger: Whippet
1972	Deborah Von Ahrens: Afghan Hound
1973	Teresa Nail: Doberman Pinscher
1974	Leslie Church: Miniature Schnauzer
1975	Virginia Westfield: Bulldog
1976	Kathy Hritzo: Samoyed
1977	Randy McAteer: Irish Setter
1978	Sonda Peterson: Boxer
1979	Susan Schneider: English Springer Spaniel
1980	Laura Mazzaro: Norweigian Elkhound
1981	Valerie Nunes: German Shorthaired Pointer
1982	Francesca Weisser: Saluki
1983	Tracie Laliberte: Lhasa Apso
1984	Brad Buttner: Great Dane
1985	David Harper: Weimaraner
1986	Wendy Rene Mattson: Doberman Pinscher
1987	Heather E. Christie: Viszla
1988	Patricia Fearing: Standard Poodle
1989	Michelle Samson: Doberman Pinscher
1990	Jessica Wiwi: Standard Poodle
1991	Kara Purcell: Afghan
1992	Christina Marley: German Wirehaired Pointer
1993	Stacy Duncan: English Springer Spanier
1994	Melanie Schlenkert: Black Cocker Spaniel
1995	Kyle Covill: Dachsund (Smooth)
1996	David Stout: Rottweiler
1997	Casandra Clark: Siberian Husky

Chapter 13

The World Series of Junior Showmanship

At the time of this writing, the future of the World Series of Junior Showmanship is uncertain. However, I feel it is important from a historical standpoint to relay my experiences and some background material on this unique event.

The World Series was created in 1988 by Newport Dog Shows and was sponsored by Pedigree® Dog Food. The finals for the World Series were held in June of each year at the Beverly Hills Kennel Club Show. The First Place Winner at this event would represent the United States at the Pedigree Chum International Junior Showmanship Competition at Crufts in Birmingham, England.

To be eligible to compete at the World Series of Junior Showmanship, it was necessary for a junior to win Best Junior Handler at one of the 22 qualifying shows. Each finalist was awarded an all-expenses-paid trip to Beverly Hills which included his dog and a chaperone.

The qualifying shows were: Santa Barbara KC (August); Waukesha KC (July); Westchester KC (September); Houston KC (August); Eugene KC (September); Westbury KC (October); Eastern KC (November); Western Reserve KC (December); Greater Daytona Dog Fanciers Association (January); Kennel Club of Beverly Hills (February); Seattle KC (February); Northern New Jersey KC (March); Detroit KC (March); Del Valle KC (March); Louisville KC (March); International KC (April); Sahuaro State KC (April); Old Dominion KC (April); Trenton KC (May); Intermountain KC (May); Evergreen Colorado KC (June); and, Framingham District KC (June).

In addition to the all-expenses-paid trip to Crufts, the First Place Junior Handler at the finals also received a personal computer and a

Anne Olejniczak winning the World Series Qualifier at the Detroit Kennel Club in 1991. (Booth Photo)

$2000 scholarship. The first and second runners-up were awarded a $1000 and a $500 scholarship respectively.

In 1991, I had won the qualifier at the Detroit Kennel Club and competed in the finals that year in Beverly Hills. The experience was different from any other Junior Handling event I had ever attended.

Pedigree and Newport Dog Shows were wonderful hosts during this special weekend. A banquet was held for the finalists and their chaperones the evening we arrived. The next day, we were treated to an all-day excursion at Magic Mountain, an elaborate amusement park. Each year, the juniors were taken to different theme parks, including Disneyland and Universal Studios.

On the final day, we attended the Beverly Hills KC Show as a group. This proved to be quite an experience. Twenty-two finalists, 22 chaperones and 22 dogs of various shapes and sizes were loaded onto two touring buses (which happened to be late). In addition, we added tack boxes, grooming tables and dog crates.

Junior Handlers in the ready ring preparing to show in the World Series Finals.

Juniors gaiting in the ring during the World Series Finals.

Stephanie Lehman winning the 1991 World Series of Junior Showmanship in Beverly Hills, California.(Bergman Photo)

Since the World Series of Junior Showmanship was not a recognized AKC event, the judging process did not have to adhere to the traditional judging format of Junior Showmanship. Judging was based not only on the handling performance of each finalist, but on the results of pre-judging interviews. Each junior was interviewed by three different judges, one was the finals judge. The interview questions centered around anatomy, your breed, handling, dog care and general dog knowledge. Regardless of how well-prepared a junior was, this portion of the competition was the most difficult. Unfortunately, as a first-time finalist this portion of the judging was not my strong point.

The handling portion of the contest was held in the Group ring prior to the start of groups. Each junior was positioned in the ring next to a placard that listed the name of the show in which he qualified. These placards were similar to the breed placards used during Group and Best in Show at Westminster. Once this handling portion of the contest was completed, the finals judge would confer with the other two judges and select the three placements.

The World Series of Junior Showmanship Winners:

1988:	Beth Rickertsen, Cocker Spaniel
1989:	Andrew Boatwright, Scottish Terrier
1990:	Kara Purcell, Afghan Hound
1991:	Stephanie Lehman, Pug
1992:	Elizabeth Schmidt, Pointer
1993:	Phil Guidry, Cocker Spaniel
1994:	Jamie Souza, Saluki
1995:	Nicole Standish

Chapter 14
Pedigree® Junior Showmanship
'National Invitational'

PEDIGREE® Food For Dogs is the sponsor for the annual PEDI-GREE® Junior Showmanship National Invitational, a competition for all junior showmanship participants. "The goal is to encourage good sportsmanship and reward natural talent of this, our next generation of breeders, owners and exhibitors. The knowledge of presentation along with proper nutrition, care and conditioning are the basics which we bestow on these youngsters who will bring our sport into the century." PEDIGREE® will send the Ultimate Winner to represent the United States at Crufts and the World Show. In addition, a scholarship will be established by PEDIGREE® in the name of the PEDIGREE® Junior Showmanship National Invitational Winner.

Twenty-one finalists will receive an all expenses paid trip to Del Mar, California to compete at the Silver Bay Kennel Club Dog Show which is held in February each year for themselves and a chaperone courtesy of PEDIGREE®. This Invitational will differ from all other previous competitions in that two winners will be chosen. The Open Junior Class Winner (at least 10 and under 14 years of age) will win an all expenses paid trip for themselves and a chaperone to compete in the Junior Showmanship Competition at the World Dog Show. Junior Handlers participating at the World Show cannot be more than

18 years of age by the date of the show because of F.C.I. age restrictions.

The winner of the Open Senior class competition (at least 14 and under 18 years of age) will win an all expenses paid trip for themselves and a chaperone to compete in the Junior Showmanship Competition at the Crufts Dog Show in Birmingham, England. Class eligibility for the Finals will be based on the date of the qualifier rather than the date of the Finals. A junior handler is eligible to win only ONE qualifier to compete at the Finals.

The Ultimate Winner from the designated quality competitions listed below will compete at the World Show.

Open Junior Class Qualifiers:

Silver Bay Kennel Club (February)
Del Mar, California

Pocatello Kennel Club (June)
Blackfoot, Idaho

Kennel Club of Beverly Hills (June)
Los Angeles, California

Greater Clark County Kennel Club (July)
Brush Prairie, Washington

Tampa Kennel Club (July)
Tampa, Florida

Westchester Kennel Club (September)
Tarrytown, New York

Heart of the Plains Kennel Club (September)
Lubbock, Texas

Westbury Kennel Club (September)
Oyster Bay, New York

Illinois Capital Kennel Club (October)
Springfield, Illinois

Kennel Club of Philadelphia (November)
Philadelphia, Pennsylvania

Central Ohio Kennel Club (November)
Columbus, Ohio

The Ultimate Winner from the designated qualifying competitions listed below will compete at the Crufts Dog Show in Birmingham, England.

Best Junior Handler Qualifiers

Golden Gate Kennel Club (February)
San Francisco, California

Westminster Kennel Club (February)
New York, New York

Silver Bay Kennel Club (February)
Del Mar, California

Del Valle Kennel Club (March)
Pleasanton, California

Evansville Kennel Club (March)
Louisville, Kentucky

International Kennel Club (March)
Chicago, Illinois

Atlanta Kennel Club (April)
Perry, Georgia

Open Senior Class Qualifiers

Old Dominion Kennel Club (April)
Leesburg, Virginia

Bucks County Kennel Club (May)
Erwinna, Pennsylvania

San Antonio Kennel Club (June)
San Antonio, Texas

Eastern Dog Club (December)
Boston, Massachusetts

Sources:

Pedigree Press Release, 1996.

Chapter 15
Crufts

In the past, Crufts was held in January; however, more recently the event is held in March in Birmingham, England. Before the introduction of the World Series of Junior Showmanship, the Best Junior Handler at Westminster was awarded an all-expenses-paid trip to compete at the Pedigree Chum International Junior Showmanship Competition held at Crufts. From 1989 to 1995, the first-place winner in the World Series of Junior Showmanship Finals represented the United States at this event. In 1996, the United States will be represented by the first winner of the Pedigree® Junior Showmanship National Invitational.

Crufts is very different from any other Junior Showmanship competition. The junior is not permitted to ship his own dog to the competition because of the six-month quarantine in England. Therefore, the juniors are given a dog on the day of the event to handle. Crufts offers many activities for the junior handler, including agility and obedience competitions.

A dinner is held for all Junior Showmanship participants on the night before the competition. The judge is introduced to all present. In an effort to further friendship between the various participants, each junior is requested to bring a gift that represents his country to exchange with another junior.

Several hours before the competition is to take place, each junior handler is asked what breed of dog he would like to exhibit in the competition. An alternate suggestion is also requested; however, there is usually no difficulty in finding an acceptable dog in the chosen breed.

The dog is introduced to the junior handler approximately one hour before judging. When judging begins, the junior handler will compete with this dog and then leave the ring. At this time, the juniors will trade dogs and enter the ring to compete once again with the new dog. The juniors will then leave the ring and switch back to their original dogs and return to the ring.

In the 1992 competition, 20 junior handlers competed representing 21 countries. A cut of six to eight juniors was made and put through the patterns once again. The judge made the final decision by choosing first, second and third place winners. That year, the three winners were awarded crystal trophies. Each participant received an engraved crystal picture frame. After the show, each junior was given a souvenir photo album with photos of the junior with the dogs, judge, other competitors and various candid poses. A video tape of the event was also sent.

Tracie Laliberte with Ch. Orlane's Intrepid winning the First International Junior Showmanship Competition held at Crufts in 1984.

Chapter 16
Special Awards for Junior Handlers

Junior Showmanship is encouraged by local all-breed clubs as well as national breed specific clubs. For instance, the American Lhasa Apso Club offers two annual awards. First, a plaque is awarded for Westminster-qualified junior handlers whose parents are members of the club. Second, a plaque is awarded to the Best Junior Handler at the National Specialty. The English Springer Spaniel Association of America presents plaques to the top Springer Junior Handler and to the runner-up.

Check with your local all-breed club or national breed club for awards offered in Junior Showmanship. If they do not offer any awards, have your parents suggest that the club begin a program for Junior Showmanship. After all, the juniors will be the future of the breed and the dog world.

The Owner Handlers Association offers trophies for the all-breed top 10 junior handlers each year who are members of the club. (See Appendix.)

The Dog Writers Association of America (DWAA) offers the annual Junior Writers Award. This award is given to juniors who have contributed to the world of dogs through their writing. A cash award and the Maxwell Riddle Medallion are awarded to the recipient.

The Junior Writers Award is presented at the DWAA Annual Awards Banquet which is usually held on the Sunday before Westminster in New York City. I had the good fortune to be the 1992 recipient of this award and attended the banquet. The members present were cordial and went out of their way to make me feel comfortable and welcome. It was a pleasure to be surrounded by so many true dog lovers and an experience I will always cherish.

Scholarships are offered through several organizations. The American Kennel Club offers veterinary scholarships and in 1994, awarded $58,000 in funds to eligible recipients. The criteria for awarding these scholarships is based on the applicants' need, academic achievement and potential, and their involvement in canine biology and the sport of purebred dogs. Scholarship amounts range from $1,000 to $3,000. For further information contact the AKC Veterinary Scholarship Department, 51 Madison Avenue, New York, New York 10010.

The Dog Writer's Educational Trust, which is sponsored by the Dog Writer's Association of America, offers scholarships to students who are enrolled in or are about to enter college. Recipients must show academic excellence and a keen interest in dog-related activities. In 1994, $10,000 in scholarships were awarded. For an application, send a self-addressed stamped envelope to Berta I. Pickett, Executive Secretary, Dog Writer's Educational Trust, P. O. Box 2220, Payson, AZ 85547-2220.

The Maxwell Riddle Medallion.

Chapter 17
Judging Junior Showmanship

When applying to AKC for a license to judge any breed, Junior Showmanship judging privileges are automatically awarded if the applicant places a check mark in the appropriate box. This lack of specific judging requirements has lead to an inconsistency in the judging of Junior Showmanship. The AKC has taken steps to improve this situation by revising and clarifying the rules, regulations and judging criteria in its booklet, *Junior Showmanship: Regulations Judging Guidelines and Guidelines for Juniors,* October 1989. In addition, retired junior handlers and other individuals active in Junior Showmanship have been encouraged to apply for Junior Showmanship judging licenses. The AKC considers their experiences ample prerequisite for application and approval.

Junior Showmanship is judged from a completely different standpoint than any other competition at a dog show. The quality of the junior's handling skills are judged rather than the quality of the dog. Therefore, the junior handler accepts full responsibility for failure or success in the Junior Showmanship ring. Understanding that this competition is of great importance to the average junior handler, it will be your responsibility to judge this event to the best of your ability. As an ex-Junior Showmanship mother, I can tell you with complete confidence that junior handlers take this competition very seriously. To most juniors, Best Junior Handler competition is as important to them as the Best in Show competition is to the professional handler. Understanding that this competition is of great importance to the average junior handler, it will be your responsibility to judge this event—a responsibility that cannot be taken lightly.

The late judge Lina Basquette awarding a first-place win.
(Booth Photo)

If you do not have the patience nor a genuine interest in Junior Showmanship, do not accept assignments. Whether you realize it or not, those young exhibitors are the hope and the future of the dog world. If you treat them indifferently or in a cavalier manner, you are not setting a good example nor giving them the encouragement they deserve.

When judging Junior Showmanship, remember it is the skill of the junior handler that is being tested not the quality or performance of the dog. Always give each junior handler the same consideration when judging skills regardless of the breed being shown, age or class. Do not be intimidated by parents or handlers standing at ringside. If you give placements to their children or protégés under duress, you are cheating every junior handler exhibiting in the ring. In addition, you are giving the recipients of your awards the impression that intimidation tactics are a normal part of dog shows and that it will not be necessary for them to know their craft to be successful. This lesson will not serve them well when they graduate from Junior Showmanship to the breed classes.

Good handling is an art. The final goal of a good handler should be to disappear behind his dog. The motions and gestures utilized to direct the dog into the assigned patterns and to keep the dog under control should be light and subtle in nature. Exaggerated movements should be faulted. The object of showing is to show the dog, not draw attention to the handler.

Each breed shown in Junior Showmanship should be presented in the same manner as the dog would be shown in the breed classes. If you are not familiar with the intricacies of showing the various breeds, study the standards or watch the various groups at shows prior to your judging assignment.

Many judges like to rearrange their classes while judging Junior Showmanship from large dogs to small dogs. When making these rearrangements make sure you do not forget the smaller dogs at the end of the line. Many times, the small dogs are placed at the end of the line and never looked at again. I have witnessed glowing performances by junior handlers with small breeds that were totally ignored. Preferences toward either size extreme should be avoided since it is the junior handler's performance that is being judged.

If a dog is fidgeting or giving a junior a difficult time by breaking stance or moving a foot, observe the junior's reaction to the situation

Heather Grodi winning Best Junior Handler under Judge Cherie Berger. (Booth Photo)

rather than eliminating him from the competition. His reaction to this difficulty is a great way of gauging handling skills. A good junior handler will not panic or become frustrated, but will restack the dog or continue to try and bring the dog under control. However, if a dog is out of control and presenting possible danger to other handlers or dogs, the dog should be excused from the ring.

The AKC Guidelines for Judging offers the following checklist for judging ring presentation:

> 1. Is the dog responsive to the handler? Do they work as a team?
>
> 2. Does the dog appear posed or interested at all times?
>
> 3. Is the dog under control?
>
> 4. Is the dog moved correctly to the best of its ability?
>
> 5. Are the dog's main faults being minimized?
>
> 6. Do both the dog and handler appear relaxed?
>
> 7. Is the dog presented with an apparent minimum effort?

The junior handler should have a working knowledge of ring procedure. "The judge shall evaluate the ability of the junior to follow directions, use space wisely, and execute the requested gaiting patterns. Juniors should appear "Ring Wise," alert to the judging progression and be prepared for changes in the judging routine." While judging, be sure that your directions are clear and concise. Be patient and considerate with the young or inexperienced junior handler. Curt words or a show of impatience can destroy what little confidence these handlers may possess. When judging the higher levels of Junior Showmanship, such as Open Senior or Best Junior Handler, request unexpected patterns or a different pattern for each junior to observe the response to a change in routine. Juniors at these levels should be well prepared for this test of their skills.

If you are approached by a junior handler for a critique after judging , be prepared to give constructive criticism on handling skills. Many juniors living in rural areas do not have access to training classes; therefore, your comments may be the only means available for them to improve their skills. Whenever possible during a critique, try to add a positive comment to the conversation regarding performances. Even the most dismal performance has to have at least one bright spot. Not only will your critique give the junior something to build on for the next show, but will leave the junior with a better feeling about himself and his performance. In large classes where it would be easy to confuse one handler with another, keep short notes of each handler's performance for reference if necessary.

Make sure your comments or suggestions are accurate and sensible. Over the years, my daughter received some very interesting answers to her inquiries. One judge told her that showing was like "polishing rocks—some's shines and some's don't." This did not offer her much to work with to improve her next performance. Another judge told her that showing a little dog (she was showing a Lhasa Apso), was much easier than showing the larger breeds. This judge had to be totally ignorant of the intricacies of showing a Lhasa. Not only do you have a full-length coat to contend with, but the Lhasa is a very independent breed. This independent spirit can make a regimented performance such as Junior Showmanship competition challenging because the dog possesses a mind of his own and often uses it. Each breed presents its own set of unique difficulties when being shown. Always make sure you treat them with equal importance, even if it is a breed with which you are not familiar.

There is a saying that "clothes make the man." When showing dogs, the handler's appearance is as important as that of his dog—together they combine to make an overall picture. A junior handler should be neat in appearance, and his dog should be clean and groomed appropriately for the breed. In the higher levels of Junior Showmanship competition many of the participants wear expensive suits and dresses. A judge should never discriminate against juniors because of the cost of their wardrobes. Always remember you are judging the junior's handling technique not his fashion sense. Do not be overly swayed by the professional look of a junior handler if the professional technique is not present. In life, many of the best things come in plain brown wrappers!

Although the emphasis of Junior Showmanship is placed on the handling portion of the competition, good sportsmanship is the foundation on which Junior Showmanship is built. Winning is a motivation for many individuals who show dogs. There is nothing wrong with this motivation as long as it remains within perspective. Winning at any cost is never an acceptable goal. Juniors should always conduct themselves in a polite and considerate manner in and out of the ring. Intentional spooking or frightening of competitors' dogs, crowding, or any other unsportsmanlike behavior while in the ring should be discouraged. Lapses in good judgment or sportsmanship should be faulted as heavily as lapses in good handling. Awarding wins or placements will only encourage the perpetrator to continue this bad behavior and is not in the best interest of the sport.

Juniors should not only be considerate of those around them, but also of their dogs. Corrections for inappropriate behavior should be light and humane. When the weather is warm, watch the junior to see if he is making sure the dog's needs are being met. Does the dog have water available? Is he keeping him in the shade when possible? Is the dog being pushed beyond his endurance because the win is all important? You should also be conscious of the dog's needs under these circumstances as well. Try not to overwork the classes in extremely hot or humid weather. Always tell the juniors not being examined to allow their dogs to rest in the shade until it is their turn. Your concern for the dog's welfare will set a good example for the juniors and will make the dogs in your ring forever grateful.

Judging Junior Showmanship is a grave responsibility. Not only are you molding the character of future breeders and handlers, but the character of our sport.

Chapter 18
Junior Showmanship in Canada

Junior Showmanship in Canada differs greatly from Junior Showmanship in the United States. The rules and regulations governing junior handling are more strict; however, they emphasize discipline while at the same time stressing the importance of enjoyment. The Canadian Kennel Club (CKC) offers many outlets for the junior handler and awards them the same respect as that of the adults exhibitors.

The Junior Kennel Club
Junior Kennel Club can be sponsored by an all-breed or specialty club and is available for those individuals who have not turned 18 years of age. Junior Kennel Club is organized in the same manner as a regular kennel club with the election of officers and business is conducted by the constitution. The members of a Junior Kennel Club are allowed to hold their own competitions and social gatherings. Sanctioned matches by recognized Junior Kennel Clubs may be held with CKC approval; however, these clubs may not hold any CKC event at a championship level. The purpose of the Junior Kennel Club is to promote education and to stress enjoyment of the sport of showing dogs.

Class Divisions
The breakdowns for the classes in junior handling in Canada varies slightly from those in the United States. Classes are divided into the following divisions:

Pee Wee: for children four to seven years of age. These classes are optional and are for exhibition only. The children are not placed as in the regular classes, but can be awarded rosettes or ribbons for participation.

Junior Novice: for junior handlers eight years of age up to and inclusive of 12 years of age. This division is reserved for those individuals who have not been awarded four first place wins in this division.

Junior Open: for junior handlers eight years of age up to and inclusive of 12 years of age. This division is reserved for those individuals who have been awarded four first place wins in Junior Novice or any handler who meets the age qualification and wishes to enter this class. A junior may not enter in the Junior Novice division once he or she has exhibited in this division.

Senior Novice: for junior handlers 13 years of age and under 18 years of age. This division is reserved for those individuals who have not been awarded four first place wins in this division.

Senior Open: for junior handlers 13 years of age and under 18 years of age who have been awarded four first place wins in Senior Novice or any handler who has exhibited as an Open Handler in either age group. Junior Handlers who have graduated from the Junior Open division by age may enter directly into this division or begin at this age level at Senior Novice.

Best Overall: this class is equivalent to Best Junior Handler in the United States and is an optional class left to the host clubs discretion.

Placing and Points Tabulation

After each junior handling competition, the Junior Kennel Club advisor or tabulator records the accumulated points for the participants. Each class consists of four placings with points awarded for each placing as follows: first place - 100 points; second - 75 points; third - 50 points; and fourth - 25 points.

The total points earned by a junior handler are recorded from January 1 to December 31. Junior handlers who compete in a province or zone in which they do not reside will have their points forwarded to their regional tabulator. In this way, a junior handler will only be able to qualify for the Best Junior Handler in one province or zone.

Provincial/Zone Junior Handling Competitions

Once a year, a competition is held in each province or zone to select the Best Junior Handler for that CKC-designated zone. The classes

Jodie Paquette, Top Junior Handler in Canada for 1993. (Alex Smith Photo)

for this division are divided into four divisions: Novice Junior, Novice Senior, Open Junior and Open Senior. The top five juniors in each division, which is decided by the total accumulated points during the calendar year, compete for Best Junior Handler in the province or zone. In the event of a tie in any of the five placings, all juniors tied for the placement will be eligible to compete.

The Provincial/Zone competition is judged by a panel comprised of a minimum of three judges. Score sheets may be kept and after the panel of judges confers with one another the finalist in each division will be chosen. The winner of each division will then compete for Top Provincial/Zone Finalist. A Reserve finalist will also be selected in the event a finalist is unable to attend the National Junior Handling Competition. All provincial/zone finals must be held no later than August 31. At the Provincial/Zone finals, the junior handler who accumulates the most points at championship shows/matches will receive the Highest Aggregate Junior Handling Award.

The National Junior Handling Competition

The winners of the Top Provincial/Zone Finals will compete for the Top Canadian Junior Handler. At this level of competition, the classes will not be divided. The judging procedure will be conducted in the same manner as the Provincial/Zone Finals. However, if the dogs being shown are of a "size and manageability," the junior handlers may be requested to exchange dogs to evaluate further their handling skills and technique.

Judging Standards

The guidelines for judging junior handling are very similar to those in the United States. The Canadian guidelines comply with those in the United States in that the dog's quality should never be judged. The handler's manner, rapport with the dog, and handling skills should be the only deciding factors.

During judging, junior handlers are to be upgraded for sportsmanlike behavior and good handling of a bad situation. Judges should be able to discern between good handling techniques and a junior who is handling a highly trained dog that shows himself. Juniors should be downgraded for making a hard correction while exhibiting in junior handling. However, the dog must always be under control and not pose a danger to any other exhibitor or dog in the ring.

Judges are encouraged to look for teamwork between handler and dog as well as the little extra that makes them shine.

Ring Procedure

The ring procedures in junior handling in Canada are relatively the same as those in the United States with a few exceptions. Courtesy turns are desirable, and judges are encouraged to have the juniors run patterns that use hand switching. Unlike in the United States, judges are permitted to ask questions and permit the exchange of dogs in the event of a tie. Junior handlers are encouraged to exhibit with a positive attitude.

Obedience Junior Handling

The Obedience Junior Handling Competition is conducted in the same manner as the Conformation Junior Handling Competition, except the junior shows the dog in the Obedience classes. Classes are offered in Novice, Open, Utility, Brace or Team as well as noncompetitive classes such as Pre-Novice and Graduate Novice.

The Obedience classes are judged on merit rather than on a passing score. Emphasis is placed on teamwork and a "smoothness and gentleness" in handling technique. The handler will be penalized for loud or harsh commands. The point system is evaluated the same as in Conformation Junior Handling.

Conclusion

The Canadian system of junior handling is an encouraging show atmosphere for the young handler. Children as young as four years of age can begin the handling and education processes. The emphasis on positive attitudes and disciplinary rules make for a future of promising, properly focused handlers.

Chapter 18
Canine Anatomy

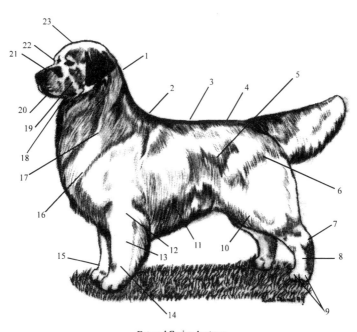

External Canine Anatomy

1. Crest	9. Digits or Toes	17. Shoulder
2. Withers	10. Stifle	18. Cheek
3. Back	11. Brisket	19. Flew
4. Hip	12. Elbow	20. Lip
5. Loin	13. Forearm	21. Muzzle
6. Point of Rump	14. Metacarpus or Pastern	22. Stop
7. Tarsus or Hock	15. Carpus or Wrist	23. Skull
8. Metatarsus	16. Point of Shoulder	

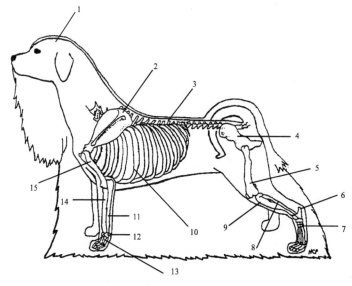

The Skeleton of the Dog

1. Occiput

2. Shoulder Blade or Scapula

3. Vertabrae

4. Pelvis

5. Femur

6. Tarsus or Hock

7. Metatarsus

8. Fibula

9. Tibia

10. Ribs

11. Ulna

12. Carpus

13. Metacarpus

14. Radius

15. Humerus or Upper Arm

Glossary

All Breed Show: The most common form of dog show that provides judging for all breeds of dogs. The dog is required to be present at the show only at the time of judging and may leave as soon as judging has been completed.

American Kennel Club (AKC): An organization that registers approved breeds of dogs and sponsors sanctions or licenses dog events.

Bait: Treats such as cooked liver, kidneys, freeze-dried liver, etc. that are used to capture the dog's attention while showing in conformation and junior showmanship.

Bait Pitching: Throwing bait in order to gain a dog's attention.

Benched Show: A dog show that has specific show hours, i.e., 9 am to 5 p.m., and the dogs must be present and on their designated benches the entire time. The only time a dog may be absent from the benching area is while being groomed, shown or excused by the superintendent.

Best Overall: At CKC-sanctioned events, a class equivalent to Best Junior Handler.

Blind Courtesy Turn: A courtesy turn in which the dog and handler move in opposite directions. Differs from a traditional courtesy turn where the handler and dog move together.

Blind Spots: Areas in the ring where calculating a judge's position are difficult.

Canadian Kennel Club (CKC): An organization that registers approved breeds of dogs and sponsors sanctions or licenses dog events.

Catalog Order: Entering the ring and lining up for class judging from the lowest to highest armband number as stated in the catalog.

Chalking: The process of using chalk to whiten or fluff up a dog's coat.

Communicable Disease: An illness that can be passed from a sick dog to healthy dogs.

Competitiveness The drive that causes an individual to give his all and with a never-quit attitude in a quest for victory.

Complimentary Picture: Presenting the judge with a clean and controlled performance.

Conformation: When a dog is being judged on conformation, the judge is evaluating the animal on his physical structure and how it adheres to the standard of the breed.

Courtesy Turn: A simple, precise 360° turn performed with dog before gaiting.

Crowding Out: A handler does not allow enough space between dogs for the next handler to show his dog effectively.

Discipline: The art of making one's self do things to benefit their handling skills. An example of discipline is regular practice sessions.

Dog Shows: An AKC-sponsored event in which all AKC-approved varieties of dogs compete in conformation, obedience and junior showmanship.

Entry Ticket: A form that contains all show information regarding the entry of dog at a specific show. Information includes the name and date of the show, dog's name, armband number, AKC number, sex, class entered, and ownership information. Many shows require this form for free admittance to the show grounds. At benched show the entry form is required for identification of the dog for admission and dismissal from the grounds.

Exaggerated Movements: Motions or gestures used by handler that draw the judge's attention away from the handler's dog.

Finer Points: The extras added to a handling performance that give it a polished, professional appearance.

Finger Works: Light hand movements used by the handler to accentuate a dog's good points.

Flat Lead: A show lead that is made of wax-coated fabric and is approximately five and one half feet in length.

Fluidity: A clean, smooth and free-flowing performance of handling a dog in conformation patterns.

Framing: The process of holding the dog's head in the right hand and resting two fingers of the left hand behind the ears.

Gaiting: The simultaneous movement of both dog and handler in a prescribed pattern that is designated by the judge.

Handling Clones: Junior handlers who show exactly alike without any defined personal style.

Heavy-handed: The use of rough corrections or movements when handling a dog.

Highest Aggregate Junior Handling Award: An award presented to the junior handler who accumulates the most points at championship shows or matches in Canada.

Individualistic: The ability to be oneself and creating own style of handling.

Judging Program: A flyer sent by a show superintendent to all exhibitors who have entered a specific show. The flyer designates the number of dogs of each sex entered in each breed, the number of junior handlers entered in each division, the time of judging and the ring number where judging will take place.

Junior Kennel Club: A club sponsored by an all-breed or specialty club in Canada that is available for individuals who have not turned 18 years of age. The club may hold its own competitions and social gatherings.

Junior Novice: At CKC-sanctioned shows, a class for junior handlers eight years of age up to and inclusive of 12 years of age. This division is reserved for individuals who have not been awarded four first place wins in this division.

Junior Open: At CKC-sanctioned shows, a class for junior handlers eight years of age up to and inclusive of 12 years of age. This division is reserved for individuals who have been awarded four first place wins in Junior Novice or any handler who meets the age qualification and wishes to enter this class. A junior may not enter in the Junior Novice division once having exhibited in this division.

Junior Showmanship: A preteen and teenage version of showing dogs in conformation at AKC events.

Junior Showmanship Identification Number: A number that is assigned to each junior handler by AKC for identification and eligibility purposes.

Martingale Choker: This lead is much like the martingale lead except that it has an attached choke collar instead of a braided collar.

Martingale Lead: A lead that is approximately five feet long and has an attached braided collar.

Mats: Removable rubber floor runners that are placed in rings at most indoor dog shows. The purpose of floor mats is to give the dog a non-slip surface on which to gait during judging.

Match: A competition similar to a dog show that is sponsored by group or kennel club. Some matches are sanctioned by AKC. The main differences between matches and regular dog shows is that judges do not have to be licensed and no championship points are awarded.

National Junior Handling Competition: In Canada, an event for the winners of the Top Provincial/Zone Finals to compete for Top Canadian Junior Handler.

Novice Junior Division: A beginners class in Junior Showmanship. Participants in this class must be 10 years of age and under 14 years of age and have not won more than three first place wins in the novice division.

Novice Senior Division: A beginners class in Junior Showmanship. Participants in this class must be 14 years of age and under 18 years of age and have not won more than three first-place wins in the novice division.

Obedience: An AKC-sponsored portion of a dog show in which the dog is evaluated by the judge on performance of the required elements for an obedience championship. To achieve an obedience championship a dog must receive three "legs," that are qualifying scores.

Obedience Junior Handling: At CKC-sanctioned events, junior handlers compete in their own division in obedience in a similar fashion to conformation Junior Handling.

Open Junior Division: A class in Junior Showmanship designed for juniors 10 years of age and under 14 years of age who have won three first-place wins in the novice division.

Open Senior Division: A class in Junior Showmanship designed for juniors 14 years of age and under 18 years of age who have won three first-place wins in the novice division.

Pattern: The gaiting formation requested by a judge in the show ring. The most common patterns are the down and back, the "L," and the triangle.

Pee Wee: At CKC-sanctioned events, a junior handling class for children four to seven years of age. These classes are optional and are for exhibition only. The children are not placed as in the regular classes, but can be awarded rosettes or ribbons for participation.

Peripheral Vision: Looking out from the corner of one's eye.

Politics: The assumption that a specific person wins because of favoritism from the judge.

Premium List: A flyer that is mailed to exhibitors by a show superintendent that announces the date, location, judging panel and entry information for a specific show or group of shows.

Provincial/Zone Junior Handling Competition: A competition held in Canada to determine the Best Junior Handler for that CKC-designated province or zone. The top five juniors in each division, decided by a total of points accumulated through the year, compete for Best Junior Handler in the province or zone.

Push-button Performance: A ring performance by a handler who has a highly trained dog and does not have to utilize handling skills to instruct the dog in the patterns.

Ready Rings: A designated area set up outside of a show ring for exhibitors and their dogs only.

Re-Stacking: Setting a dog up into a stacked position after he has broken position.

Ribbon Lead: A lead that is made of a woven, ribbon-like material approximately four feet in length. This lead is available in three different widths: one-quarter inch, three-eighths inches and five-eighths inches.

Ring Procedure: The manner in which a judge conducts the classes he is judging.

Ring Wise: A handler's ability to know how ring procedures are to be run.

Running Up: A handler or dog stepping on or running into the exhibitor or the dog ahead.

Senior Novice: At CKC-sanctioned events, a class for junior handlers 13 years of age and under 18 years of age. This division is reserved for those individuals who have not been awarded four first-place wins in this division.

Senior Open: At CKC-sanctioned events, a class for junior handlers 13 years of age and under 18 years of age who have been awarded four first-place wins in Senior Novice or any handler who has exhibited as an Open Handler in either age group. Junior Handlers who have graduated from the Junior Open division by age may enter directly into this division or begin at this age level at Senior Novice.

Show Groom: Preparation of the dog's coat that is performed at a dog show before judging. The dog must be groomed in the same way he would be groomed for showing in conformation.

Show Lead: A special leash, usually consisting of a one-piece collar and lead combination, that is used to show a dog in conformation.

Simple or Training Method of Showing: Performing patterns without courtesy turns.

Specials Dog: A dog that has completed his championship in the conformation classes and is shown in Best of Breed, Group and Best in Show.

Specialty Show: A dog show dedicated to only one breed and only dogs of that specific breed may be entered in the classes.

Stamina: The dog's ability to endure the physical and mental stresses of being shown without becoming tired.

Strung Up: A dog that is gaited on a short, tight lead and in many cases so tightly that the front feet do not touch the ground.

Superintendent: The official AKC-approved organizer of a dog show.

Switching Hands: The act of moving the lead from one hand to the other so the dog may be gaited on the opposite side of the handler. Switching hands prevents the handler from coming between his dog and the judge during patterns.

Swivel or Toy Lead: A lead that is made of a thin, floss-like material. This type of lead is used for toy dogs and dogs that are well-behaved because of the flimsy construction of the lead.

Teamwork: The ability of a junior handler and dog to work as one during a handling routine.

Traditional Method of Showing: Performing patterns with courtesy turns.

Training Class: Classes sponsored most commonly by kennel clubs that teach exhibitors how to show their dogs in conformation, obedience or junior showmanship.

Upstaging: Attempting to outshine the competition by psyching out your fellow exhibitors or by the use of over-handling.

Westminster Kennel Club Show: A dog show held in New York City at Madison Square Garden the second week of February. A junior handler must have eight or more first place wins in Open Junior Showmanship competition to be eligible to enter and compete at this event.

Bibliography

The American Kennel Club, *Junior Showmanship: Regulations for Judging Guidelines and Guidelines for Juniors*, amended October 10, 1989.

The American Kennel Club: A Source Book, *Junior Showmanship*, Korzenik, Andrea D., New York, 1985, p 167.

American Kennel Club, *Show Awards*, April 1979 to April 1996.

Brown, Marsha Hall and Mason, Bethny, *The New Complete Junior Showmanship Handbook*, Howell, 1979

The Canadian Kennel Club, *Junior Kennel Club Guidelines*, January 1, 1993.

Carlson, Delbert G., and James M. Griffin, *Dog Owner's Home Veterinary Handbook*, New York: Howell, 1992.

Crossley, A. P. C., "Dressage," *The Encyclopedia of the Horse*, New York: Crescent, p 95.

Elliott, Rachel Page, *The New Dog Steps*, Howell, 1983, p 22.

Grey, Gail L., Grey, Gene W., and Mr. Norris, Slide Show on Showing the German Shepherd.

Interview with Stephanie Lehman, 1992 International Junior Showmanship Competition participant representing the United States.

New Webster's Dictionary and Thesaurus, 1992.

Pedigree® Press Release, 1996.

Siegel, Mordecai, "Happy Birthday," *The American Kennel Gazette*, February, 1995.

Strattan, Charles, "Glossary," *The Encyclopedia of the Horse*, New York: Crescent, p 245.

Wagner, Alice M., *Popular Dogs*, February, 1968, p 35.

World Series of Junior Showmanship Press Information.

<u>Appendix</u>

The American Kennel Club (General Information)
51 Madison Avenue
New York, New York 10010
Phone: 212-696-8200 (Main switchboard)

The American Kennel Club (Registration Matters)
5580 Centerview Drive
Raleigh, NC 27606
Phone: 919-233-9767

The Canadian Kennel Club
100-89 Skyway Avenue
Etobicoke, Ontario
Canada M9W 6R4

American Kennel Club Gazette
Official Publication of the American Kennel Club
5580 Centerview
Raleigh, NC 27690-0643
Phone: 919-233-9780
Yearly Subscription Fee: $28

Dog Fancy
Subscription Department
P. O. Box 53264
Boulder, CO 80323-3264
Phone: 303-666-8504
Yearly Subscription Fee: $25.97

Dog World Magazine
29 North Wacker Drive
Chicago, IL 60606-3298
Phone: 312-726-2802
Yearly Subscription Fee: $28

Owner Handlers Association
Mrs. Mildred Mesch
6 Michaels Lane
Old Brookville, NY 11545

Dog Writers Association of America
Mordecai Siegel
55 Bethune Street
#C 614
New York, NY 10014

Annually Licensed Show Superintendents:

Antypas, William G.
P. O. Box 7131
Pasadena, CA 91109

Bradshaw, Jack
P. O. Box 7303
Los Angeles, CA 90022

Brown, Margery
P. O. Box 494665
Redding, CA 96049

Crowe, Thomas J.
P. O. Box 22107
Greensboro, NC 27420

Houser, M. Helen
P. O. Box 420
Quakertown, PA 18951

McNulty, Eileen
Route 78
Java Center, NY 14082

Mathews, Ace H.
P. O. Box 86130
Portland, OR 97286-0130

Onofrio, Jack
P. O. Box 25674
Okalhoma City, OK 73125

Peters, Bob
P. O. Box 579
Wake Forest, NC 27588

Robert Reed
177 Telegraph road
Suite 405
Bellingham, WA 98226

Roberts, Lewis
P. O. Box 4658
Federal Way, WA 98063

Rogers, Kevin B.
P. O. Box 230
Hattiesburg, MS 39403

Sleeper, Kenneth A.
P. O. Box 828
Auburn, IN 46706-0828

Wilson, Nancy
8307 E. Camelback Road
Scottsdale, AZ 85251

Zimmerman, Kathleen
P. O. Box 6898
Reading, PA 19619

Index